# YOU SHOULD KNOW THIS!

## A Rabbi Explains Christianity to Jews

By Stephen M Wylen

ISBN 978-1-66786-917-9 (print)
ISBN 978-1-66786-918-6 (eBook)

You have been shown, O mortals, what is good, and what God requires of you: only to do justice, to love graciously, and to walk humbly with your God.

- Micah 6:8

Dedicated to Avi, Ella, Shemaiah, Micah, Liliann, Kedem, Oz Yosef, Tiferet and Shalev.

And in memory of Ronin Shaiah.

May you experience a world where every person sees and reveres the image of God in every other person.

**YOU SHOULD KNOW THIS!**

**TABLE OF CONTENTS**

# INTRODUCTION TO MY JEWISH READERS

You want to know more about Christianity. This is understandable. As an English speaking Jew you live surrounded by Christians. You are personally acquainted with many Christians. You probably have many Christian friends. If you are like most American Jews then you have Christians in your extended family at this point. You may be married to a Christian. Even if you live in a fairly insular Jewish community you are surrounded by the culture of Christianity. It is in the television shows that are aired, the perspective from which social studies are taught from Kindergarten through college, in the shopping malls especially during the month of December.

A fish needs to know about the sea in which it swims. Jews in the Western world swim in an ocean of Christianity. It behooves us to understand Christians and the Christian religion.

The Jewish religion has evolved during the past two thousand years in close relationship with Christianity. Our common Scriptural heritage, our rivalry, the persecutions we have endured at the hands of Christians often inspired by their religion, our conversations and debates with our Christian neighbors, have all shaped our Jewish identity. Jews may sometimes like to think that we are entirely self-referential, but an objective look at our history tells us that the Judaism we know is unimaginable except in relation to Christianity. The Judaism that might have evolved out of ancient biblical religion without the existence of Christianity is a Judaism that is unknowable and unimaginable. A self-aware Jewish person must recognize then that we will know our own selves better if we know more about Christianity.

Sometimes Jews like to think that since "we came first" we don't have to know much about Christianity to be Jews, while since Christians came after us they need to understand Judaism to understand themselves. We will explore this issue in some depth, but suffice it to say for now that an objective view of Jewish history tells us that influence runs in both directions.

A faithful Jew who wants to learn more about Christianity has a difficult problem – to whom can one turn as a teacher? A Jew might be reluctant to ask a Christian for information for a number of good reasons. The Christian teacher might hear the request for information as an invitation to convert his or her Jewish friend to Christianity. After all, Christianity is a famously missionary religion, and Jews have been at the center of Christian missionary focus. A Jew might be concerned that a Christian teacher will teach Christianity from his or her own unique Christian perspective, leaving out other Christian points of view that could be equally important and perhaps more mainstream. A Jew might fear that a Christian friend who is happy to share information is more enthusiastic than informed, and might not be correct. A Christian who teaches from a Christian point of view might not be aware of how his or her words are heard and perhaps misunderstood by a Jewish student. Especially because Christians are so much in the majority, they might not understand the questions and issues of a Jew. For example, Christmas time is a time of great joy for many Christians and they find it hard to understand why Jews cannot simply celebrate the holiday and rejoice along with them. For these and other reasons, a Jew might be reluctant to learn more about Christianity from a Christian teacher.

A Jew also has reason to think twice before learning about Christianity from a Jewish teacher. The Jewish teacher might be more interested in immunizing the student from Christian missionary outreach than in teaching about Christianity. A Jewish teacher's point of view might be skewed by the unfortunate history of Christian persecution of Jews, leaving the teacher angry and judgmental. It is best to learn a subject from a teacher who has a passion for that subject, or at least a positive appreciation.

A Jew who wishes to learn about Christianity in our times has much to fear from Christian missionaries who pose as Jews. These missionaries might belong to the organizations Jews for Jesus or Messianic Judaism. They might even sincerely believe themselves to be Jews, but their religion is a form of Fundamentalist Christianity. They believe Judaism to be an empty, incomplete and non-salvational religion unless belief in Jesus is added to it. In this sense, despite their love for Israel and the Jewish people, they maintain and foment anti-Semitic stereotypes of the Jewish religion. These missionaries are always looking for an opportunity to interact with Jews in the hope of bringing them to Christianity, and they often misrepresent themselves as people who practice Judaism – or, as they call it in their own lingo, "completed" Judaism.

Let me assure my readers then that I, the writer of this book, am not a Christian missionary in public or in secret. I am a faithful Jew and a rabbi of the Jewish people, educated and ordained by the Hebrew Union College – Jewish Institute of Religion. Throughout my career and at present I have served as religious leader of Jewish congregations.

My own attitude to Christianity is one of positive appreciation. As much as I am glad to be a Jew, I am glad that Christians are Christian. As a student of history my eyes are open about the often unfortunate aspects of Christian-Jewish relations, but I believe that the murderous secular ideologies of the modern age have demonstrated that Jews are better off when our Christian neighbors are faithful to their own traditions. Furthermore, I am heartened by the positive transformation that many Christian denominations have made out of their own horror at the Holocaust and their regret for the persecutions of the past. In my own life I have taken pleasure and grown in wisdom and spirit from my participation in interfaith activities with my Christian neighbors. I am moved when I visit Christian worship services by the love for God that I experience in their midst. I am moved to prayer as a Jew when I experience the prayers of Christians and persons of other faiths as well. Worship, prayer, a passion to serve God, and an ethical religious impulse are not the property of any one religion; they are human traits.

I learned about a rabbi in Poland who lived at the time when electricity was being introduced to cities. He would not allow the electric wires to be brought to his synagogue when he learned that the same wires would run to the churches in his city. I am sympathetic to the feelings of that rabbi in light of the pre-Holocaust relationship between Polish Jews and Christians at the time. I am glad that we live in different times, when Jews and Christians can understand and appreciate one another. I am glad that I can enjoy the benefits of electricity running to my home without worry about who is sharing those benefits.

In olden times there were Jewish scholars who knew a lot about Christianity. Isaac Abravanel, for example, the leader of all the Jews of Spain before the Expulsion of 1492, was as learned in Christian theology as he was in Jewish teachings. Such persons were rare. A Jew had much to fear from asking about Christianity. If he did not convert after inquiring to know more about Jesus or Christianity his teachers could be offended and his life could be in danger. We are grateful that for the past two centuries, in enlightened parts of the world, Jews and Christians have been free to learn about each others' religion objectively while maintaining their own faith. Scholars of early Christian origins and scholars of the origins of Rabbinical Judaism eventually learned, through sharing their studies, that these were not two separate topics but the same topic. Jews can be enriched in our own religion by learning more about

Christianity in a spirit of free inquiry. I am honored to do my part to advance this agenda.

Because I have studied quite a bit about the historical Jesus, I am often asked by Christians how I could do this without becoming a Christian believer myself. My response is that "Judaism provides me the answer to all of my religious questions." We will talk more in a later chapter about why this is the best response to the question.

For a Jew to have a meaningful Jewish understanding of Christianity it helps to know a lot about Judaism. Many Christians have also come to understand that their own Christianity is deepened by an understanding of the Jewish background to Christianity. There is a lot of teaching about Judaism in this book, which is necessary to our purpose. I hope that my Jewish readers will find this book to be a valuable stop on your own Jewish journey.

This book is not intended to be a comprehensive scholarly introduction to Christianity. The purpose is to clear up misunderstandings and respond to urgent questions that Jews have about Christianity – from a Jewish point of view.

# INTRODUCTION TO MY CHRISTIAN READERS

Welcome to these pages. You may be reading this book to learn more about your own religion, but I suspect that your primary motivation is curiosity about what Jews think of Christianity. This book is a conversation between a Jewish rabbi and his Jewish readers. I invite any and all Christians to eavesdrop on this conversation. I think you will learn something about Jews and about your own self and your own faith in the process. I hope that mutual respect between Christians and Jews will increase as a result of this work.

It is possible that you will find some of the things said in this book to be incorrect. You may even object to some of the things that are stated. There are two main reasons for this. One is that in this work we generalize about what Christians believe and practice. Since there is much variation in Christianity, it is possible that a particular statement about Christian beliefs is not consistent with what you believe or what your denomination teaches. We will try to stay in the mainstream in describing Christian thought, but it is not possible to account for every variation. The other reason is that this is a book written by a Jew, for Jews. Sometimes Jews have a perspective on Christianity which is not consistent with what Christians say of themselves. Where this is the case we will attempt to respectfully explain the differing points of view, but we do not apologize for taking a Jewish stance. It is also possible that the writer is simply wrong about Christianity, but the manuscript of this book has been reviewed by Christian scholars in an attempt to minimize error. It should also be understood that this book accepts the findings of scientific historical study about the Bible, Judaism and Christianity. As such, one who holds a Fundamentalist or Jewishly Orthodox view of divinely ordained religion may object to aspects of my presentation. I nevertheless hope that Fundamentalist Christians and Orthodox Jews will read this book, regardless of your disagreements, for the sake of the wisdom that you might glean which could be valuable in your own journey of spirit through the world of God's making.

In the very nature of this work it is not all objective scholarship. There is room for analysis and opinion. The author takes full responsibility for my own point of view. If you choose to disagree with me, you are free to do so. Maybe someday we can meet and have a chat about our differences of opinion. If we do, I am sure I will learn from you.

The author of this book is a faithful Jew who has great respect for Christianity and for faithful Christians. I hope that my faithfulness and my respect shine through on these pages. May it all be for the greater glory of God.

# CHAPTER ONE: WHAT IS CHRISTIANITY?

The Christian religion is about two thousand years old. It is the most widespread religion on earth. Christianity is the dominant religion in Europe, North and South America, sub-Saharan Africa, Australia, South Korea and the Philippines. There are many Christians in other areas of the world as well. There are about one and a half billion Christians in the world. There are more Christians than adherents of any other religion in the world, followed by Muslims and Hindus and Buddhists. To followers of other religions who wonder why there are so many Christians, we must begin by acknowledging that there is something about Christianity that is immensely attractive to human beings and which gives Christianity a great and enduring hold on its followers.

There are numerous streams of Christianity with differing organizational hierarchies and differing beliefs. The Christians that an American Jew are mostly likely to meet fall into two major groups, Catholic Christians and Protestant Christians. The denominations of Protestant Christians are too numerous to count. An American Jew may have heard of Episcopalians, Lutherans, Baptists, Methodists, Presbyterians, Reformed, Congregationalists (United Church of Christ), Assemblies of God, among others. Mormons might be counted as Protestants or as a separate stream of Christianity. Besides Catholics and Protestants. The third very large stream of Christianity is Orthodox Christianity. There are Greek Orthodox, Russian Orthodox, Syrian Orthodox, and other Orthodox churches. There are not so many Orthodox Christians in America, but Orthodox Christianity is historically the predominant form in Eastern Europe and areas of the Middle East. There are other streams of Christianity less well known to Americans, such as Armenian Christianity, Coptic Christianity which is most common in Egypt, and other ancient Middle Eastern Churches. As this work is written with American Jews in mind, we will speak mainly about Catholic and Protestant Christianity, while remembering the existence of these other forms.

American Jews are often confused by the words Catholic and Christian, perhaps because they both begin with the letter "C". The word Christian includes all form of Christianity. The word Catholic refers to a particular branch of Christianity, the largest in the world. Catholic Christians are led by priests. The Catholic Church is well organized into a hierarchy. Priests fall under the regional leadership of bishops. All bishops fall under the leadership of the bishop of Rome, who is called the Pope. The Pope is the world leader of all Catholic Christians.

The religious leaders of Protestant Christians are called ministers, not priests. Protestant churches may have national organizations with bishops, but they are generally not as hierarchically organized as the Catholic Church. Each Protestant congregation has a fair amount of independence. While priests do not marry, Protestant ministers generally do marry and have families. Episcopalian clergy are called priests, but may marry. Catholic priests are usually distinguished by black garments, but ministers and priests cannot always be distinguished by their clothing, especially in contemporary America.

All Christians, whether Catholic, Protestant, Orthodox or other, are united by a set of basic beliefs that unites them as Christians.

The Christian religion is centered on the person Jesus of Nazareth, whom Christians call the Christ. (The meaning of this word Christ will be explained later in this book.) Christians believe, with some variation, that Jesus is the incarnation of God. That means Jesus was a human being but Jesus was also God. Christians believe that God became human in order to die as a sacrifice to atone (make up) for human sins. A Christian acquires this atonement, this forgiveness of all sins, through

14

faith. The Christian must affirm the truth of the basic Christian beliefs about the identity and purpose of Jesus Christ. A Christian who does so is "saved" – that is, this Christian person has gained forgiveness of sins and acquired eternal life in heaven. This is the goal of the Christian. The Christian religion is summarized in one often-quoted verse from the Christian Scriptures: For God so loved the world that he gave his one and only Son, that whoever believes in him shall not perish but have eternal life. (John 3:16)

It is a historical belief of Christianity that faith in Jesus as the Christ is not only a pathway to salvation, it is the only pathway to salvation. Christians feel a strong humanitarian urge to bring all other human beings to faith in the Christ so that they too may be saved. Christianity is thus an "evangelical" religion. That is, Christians feel they have a mission to bring Christianity to all the peoples of the earth. Later in this book we will explore misunderstandings that result from different Jewish and Christian views about missionary religion. For now, let us acknowledge that Christian evangelism is basic to the religion and derives from noble motives but has often brought Christians into conflict with Jews and, in a very different way, with Muslims who also feel a religious obligation to convert the world. The place of Jews as a third party in the conflict between Christendom and Islam is essential to the role and sense of identity of Jews over the past fifteen centuries.

Put simply, Christians are people who believe that faith in Jesus Christ as their Lord and Savior is the path to Salvation. In the course of this book we will come to a deeper understanding of the meaning of the words in this statement.

# CHAPTER TWO: WHO IS JESUS?

The central figure in Christianity is Jesus of Nazareth. Jesus is a Greek form of the name Yehoshua, "Joshua." Sometimes this name is shortened in Hebrew to Yeshua. Nazareth is a small village in the Galilee hill region in northern Israel. Jesus was raised in Nazareth by his family parents Mary (Miriam) and Joseph, a carpenter. In the time of Jesus, the Galilee was peopled with small villages of Aramaic speaking Jews, and the larger Greek speaking towns of Sepphoris, not far from Nazareth, and Tiberias, on the Sea (really lake) of Galilee. Those towns were populated with non-Jewish people. In the course of his public preaching career Jesus visited the various Jewish towns in the Galilee and along the shoreline of the lake, apparently avoiding the Greek cities.

American Jews are most likely to be familiar with the birth story of Jesus, due to the popularity of Christmas. This story is told, with some variations, in two books of the Christian Bible. These stories are not historically verifiable, but each detail is meant to teach a lesson that is important to Christian beliefs.

As the story is told, while Mary was pregnant with Jesus she and Joseph went to Bethlehem, a town south of Jerusalem, to be enrolled in a census. The purpose of this placement is to connect Jesus with King David, the founder of the Jewish royal dynasty, who was born and raised in Bethlehem. There was no room in any inn, so Mary and Joseph stayed in a manger, a stable for animals. Jesus' birth in a manger represents his rise to greatness from humble origins. A great star, probably representing a constellation of planets, appeared in the sky. This motif is usual in the ancient birth stories of great persons. A similar star appears in the sky in the Jewish birth legend of Father Abraham, from the same time period, as found in midrash Genesis Rabbah. Shepherds from round about saw the star and were told its significance by an angel. They came to visit the child. In another version it is non-Jewish wise men, in later legend identified as kings, who came to visit. The shepherds are Jewish, while the kings symbolizes that Christianity is to be a world religion, not limited to Jewish followers. We are not saying that any of these events did or did not happen, only that the way the story is told is meant to teach certain Christian lessons.

The virgin birth of Jesus is part of the story. It is told that Mary was a virgin who had never had sex with a man. She became pregnant through a divine miracle. Her pregnancy was told to her, and explained to Joseph, by angels of God. The annunciation of Mary's miraculous pregnancy is patterned on the story of the annunciation of Sampson in the biblical Book of Judges. The idea of a virgin birth generally strains the imagination of Jews. Virgin birth stories were common in the Greek and Roman society that surrounded the Jewish world. A virgin birth story would have been acceptable in that society. It is likely that the belief in the virgin birth of Jesus originally arose amongst early Gentile Christians, while early Jewish Christians would have insisted on Jesus' royal descent through his father Joseph. Such a royal geneology is provided in the Gospel of Matthew. The crown of Israel is transmitted only through the male line. In the end both of these motifs are included in the birth story.

The birth story of Jesus is lovely. It captures the imagination of Christians, and even Jews cannot help but be moved by it. After the birth stories, with their legendary quality, we know nothing about Jesus' childhood and upbringing until the beginning of his public preaching career. The Gospel of Luke tells a story of the boy Jesus amazing the scholars of Judaism with his erudition, but this story stands alone and is not consistent with the stories of Jesus' adult life.

Jesus grew up quietly in Nazareth. Jesus would be known to his neighbors as the son of Mary and of Joseph, the carpenter. Presumably Jesus would have apprenticed to his father and learned carpentry. When he was about 31 years old, Jesus went down to the Jordan River to see John, whom Christians call John the Baptist. John was immersing people in the Jordan River. Immersion, "mikvah", is a Jewish ritual of purification. John extended the meaning of mikvah as a symbol of spiritual and ethical renewal. John himself lived a simple life by the Jordan River, wearing rough clothing and eating wild food, locusts and honey, after the manner of the biblical prophet Elijah. John became popular with urban Jews from Jerusalem and elsewhere, who flocked to him to be immersed.

Jesus' immersion by John caused a spiritual awakening in him. Upon his return to the Galilee he began a public career of preaching. His preaching focused on the need for a radical transformation of one's life in preparation for the immanent coming of the Kingdom of God. The Kingdom of God was a biblical idea that evolved into new forms among Jews in the Roman Era. It came to mean that God would overturn the Roman Empire and directly rule over a remade world.

Jesus' preaching attracted crowds of the common folk, particularly in the fishing villages along the shore of the Kinneret, the Sea of Galilee. Jesus acquired an inner circle of devoted disciples. Jesus' most intimate followers are remembered as the Twelve Apostles. The number twelve is symbolic of the Twelve Tribes of Israel, meant to represent the totality of the Jewish nation.

After a year, or possibly two years, of public preaching in the Galilee, Jesus made a pilgrimage to Jerusalem for the Passover holiday, accompanied by his closest disciples. It was a goal of every Jew in the Roman Empire to visit Jerusalem for the holiday of Passover at least once in a lifetime. The city was crowded with pilgrims. At the Passover season the Roman rulers of Judea, who maintained their own capital in Caesarea by the Mediterranean Sea, reinforced the guard in Jerusalem in order to keep the peace. In Jesus' time, the Roman governor of Judea was Pontius Pilate. The High Priest, Caiphas, was the internal Jewish ruler of Judea.

Jesus attracted the attention of the authorities with his public preaching, and also because in his outrage at the commercial atmosphere that surrounded the Temple, especially at the festival time, he overturned the tables of the money-changers. The money-changers were present in the Temple courtyard so that foreign visitors could acquire Temple coinage for donations and for the purchase of sacrificial animals. Just after Jesus and his followers had observed the Passover feast according to the custom of the times, or perhaps on the day before, Jesus was arrested by the Temple guard. Jesus was taken to hearings before the High Priest and the Sanhedrin, the Jewish high court. He was then taken before his own ruler Herod Junior, king of Galilee, who was in Jerusalem for the Passover holiday. Ultimately Jesus was taken before Pontius Pilate, the Roman governor of Judea. Pontius Pilate sentenced Jesus to death by crucifixion, a tortuous way to die which the Romans reserved for those accused of crimes against the State. The probable reason for the death sentence is that preaching the coming Kingdom of God was seditious against the Roman rulers. Later Christians may have seen Jesus' Kingdom of God as taking place on a spiritual plane, not relevant to earthly rule, but such a distinction would not have been known nor made a difference to the Romans.

After Jesus' death, his followers were originally deeply discouraged, but they came to believe that Jesus had fulfilled his mission precisely by dying on the cross. Thus did Christianity come into being.

The Gospels tell that on the third day after Jesus' death on the cross he arose from the dead and returned to his original source in Heaven. The belief in resurrection of the dead was controversial in Jesus' time; it was central to the Judaism of the Pharisees, the forerunners of rabbinical Judaism. Christians claimed that prior to the general resurrection of the dead, which the Pharisees taught would come at the end of time, Jesus had been individually resurrected. The Gospels say that on the third day various persons went to the tomb where Jesus was buried. There they saw that the stone which covered the tomb had rolled away, and the tomb was empty.

The story of Jesus' arrest, trial, crucifixion and resurrection is called by Christians "the Passion." The Passion story is the earliest core of the life story of Jesus told in the four Gospels of the Christian Bible. The rest of Jesus' life story was reconstructed by the Gospel writers backwards, from his death to his birth. The Passion narrative is central to the Christian faith.

Christians learn the reported words of Jesus from the New Testament Gospels, which generates in the reader the impression that Jesus' words were original to him. Jews who study the life and the preaching of Jesus of Nazareth find many points of intersection with Jewish teachings. Before we conclude that Jesus learned his teachings from rabbinic sources, we must recall that our rabbinic texts were composed and edited in their final form quite some time after the time of Jesus. It is not so easy to say who came first. Many of the themes of Jesus' and the rabbinic Sages' teachings were part of the universal heritage of Hellenistic Judaism. Jewish and Christian scholars debate the extent of Jesus' originality. It is my opinion that this question is only meaningful when applied over and over to each specific teaching. There is no one answer.

The Passion narrative is also relevant to Jews. Jews have a great stake in the interpretation of this story, since Jews have been held to account for Jesus' death, with dire consequences for the Jewish people. After Jesus' death on the cross, the story of his resurrection belongs to the world of Christian belief. That is where Christianity parts company with Judaism and becomes a different religion. That is the point where the Jewish man, Jesus of Nazareth, becomes the Christian Christ.

# CHAPTER THREE: JESUS THE CHRIST

The Christian religion is not based on what Jesus preached but on the meaning of Jesus' death by crucifixion and reported resurrection. Who is Jesus to Christians? Why did he die as he did? Jesus himself did not preach Christianity, which makes him unique amongst religious founders. Christianity is not based on what Jesus said but on who Jesus was.

Jesus' circle of followers probably expected him to bring about the Kingdom of God, God's direct rule over the earth, in his lifetime, by calling down the miraculous power of God into earthly affairs. Jesus' death was a shock to his disciples, who scattered in dismay. They quickly came to believe that Jesus had not failed in his mission by dying, but succeeded in his mission. This required a new understanding of Jesus' life and death, an understanding that resulted in the new religion of Christianity.

We know virtually nothing about the evolution of Christianity in the fifteen or so years immediately following the crucifixion of Jesus, in about the year 33 CE. We would love to know, but there are no sources. When the young Christian religion appears on the scene some years later, we find a small and devoted circle of Christian followers who believe that Jesus died to bring about the Kingdom of God in a heavenly realm that would soon be expressed on earth. To Christians, the growth of Christianity from a small group of discouraged followers to an expanding world religion is a miraculous demonstration of the truth of Christianity. To non-Christians it is a cause for wonder. Jesus and his followers spoke Aramaic. The Christian Church that appears on the scene some years later is Greek speaking and includes many Gentiles. How did this transformation take place?

In its earliest years Christianity was a sect within Judaism, at a time when there were many Jewish sects. The Christian sect had some distinctive beliefs, but in order to be a Christian one had to be a Jew. As Christianity spread amongst Gentiles the connection to Judaism became tenuous and soon was broken entirely. Christianity became a separate and distinct religion which spread in the Greek and Latin speaking Gentile world. Those Jews who had been part of the early Christian Church quickly ceased to identify as Jews and became Gentiles themselves.

After some early debates about who Jesus really was and the meaning of his death, Christians came to call Jesus the Christ. Christ is a Greek word with its own Christian meaning, but Christians often use the Jewish term Messiah as a synonym for Christ. We will discuss later why this comparison may be misleading. Let us for now discuss the meaning of the Christian term Christ without reference to the Jewish Messiah.

The Christ is God become human. Through a process that Christians call "incarnation", God causes a virgin woman to become pregnant and God is born as a human being. This person then dies as a perfect sacrifice to atone for all human sins. Those who believe that Jesus is truly the Christ share in the atoning value of his sacrifice and are granted the salvation of their souls, meaning that all their sins are forgiven and they may enter Heaven upon their death. For Christians, Jesus Christ is Lord and Savior, meaning their heavenly ruler and the one who guarantees entry into Heaven for their souls.

Jews who are not familiar with Christian faith may think that Jesus Christ is Jesus' full name. Actually, Jesus' name is Jesus of Nazareth. Christ is a title granted to Jesus, expressing Christian faith in the meaning of his life and death.

The doctrine of the Christ may seem alien to Jews for a number of reasons. Jews believe that God is always God and humans are always human. The idea of a divine human seems strange to Jews, and we may wonder how others believe it. For Jews, salvation based on what one believes rather than how one behaves (mitzvah) may seem foreign. For Christians, salvation through Christ is an act of pure divine grace that cannot be earned or achieved. Jews, by contrast, are comfortable with the idea of acquiring merit and then allowing God to make up the difference. The midrash asks, what mitzvah did the Jews perform to give God an opening to redeem them from slavery in Egypt? For Christians, the mitzvot of the redeemed would be beside the point. For Jews, the idea of salvation has a national and communal component; it is not primarily about the saving of one's own soul. Finally, and perhaps most significant, Jews do not believe that the human soul is in need of transformation through faith. Jews believe that the soul is created pure, and can be improved and even perfected through education in Torah.

Imagine if you will one of those Easter period television shows about the life of Jesus. The scene begins with a close-up of Jesus, then telescopes out to the large enthusiastic crowd of listeners. Then the camera shot falls back to two Roman soldiers keeping watch over the crowd and wondering at Jesus' preaching. One soldier says to his fellow, "Could this person be the Christ that the Jews have been waiting for?" The movie might perhaps quote the New Testament: "Truly, this was the son of God." (Matt. 27:54/Mark 15:39)

This scene, or something like it, is commonly understood by many of today's Christians to be accurate. It suggests that the doctrine of the Christ existed within First Century Judaism, waiting for Jesus to come and fulfill the expectations. Jesus is seen as the peg that fit perfectly into the hole in the center of Judaism. Even the Romans knew about it.

This idea is historically inaccurate. The doctrine of the Christ developed after the crucifixion of Jesus, to explain the Christian meaning of his death. The belief that the doctrine of the Christ predates Jesus is insulting to Judaism, even if unintentionally, because it suggests that the Jews were waiting for Christ and yet refused to accept him when he arrived. That would indeed make Jews stubborn and foolish. This belief is responsible for the confusion of many Christian persons about why Jews do not come to Jesus and accept Christianity.

If a Jewish person wishes to understand Christianity then we must accept that Judaism and Christianity are different religions with different ideas and beliefs about God and about humankind. Even though Christianity has its earliest origins within Judaism, the two religions evolved in different directions. The doctrine of the Christ, the divine human who suffers death as an atonement for human sins and provides salvation through faith in him, is the central belief that distinguishes Christianity from Judaism and all other religions.

# CHAPTER FOUR: PAUL, THE FOUNDER OF CHRISTIANITY?

The doctrine of the Christ was developed and explained by Paul, an early exponent of Christianity who is the author and subject of much of the Christian Bible, the New Testament. Paul explains how the doctrine of the Christ distinguishes Christianity from historical Judaism. He often contrasts Christianity and Judaism in stark terms. Paul also created the Gentile Church. He was the first to say that a Gentile who wished to become a Christian did not have to first convert to Judaism. He allowed Gentiles to become Christian without circumcision and without observing the kosher food laws. He eliminated the observance of mitzvot, divine commandments, for Christians, with the exception of the Ten Commandments.

For these reasons, Jewish historical scholars of Christianity in the Nineteenth Century identified Paul as the first Christian and the founder of Christianity. These scholars chose to reclaim Jesus of Nazareth for Judaism, most likely as a way of raising the stature of contemporary Jews in an atmosphere of rising European anti-Semitism.

Christian scholars are aware that Jews identify Paul rather than Jesus as the first Christian, and many are not especially fond of that point of view. Historical scholars would admit that Jesus in his public career did not have a developed concept of Christianity and was not seeking to found a new religion, but they would still argue that Jesus surely has something to do with the foundations of Christianity.

Although I wish to be sensitive to Christian feelings, I must admit that I share the judgment of the early modern Jewish scholars that Jesus was a Jew, while Paul was a Christian and, in the fully developed sense, perhaps the first Christian. Jesus' original followers and the earlier Church must surely be seen as proto-Christians, but the beliefs that distinguish Christianity from Judaism had not yet come into being.

Paul began his public career as an anti-Christian preacher. He was a disciple of Gamaliel, head of the nascent rabbinical council. Paul sought to suppress the Christian heresy within Judaism. As the Pharisees consolidated their hold on Jewish leadership, they ceased to be a sect. Their leaders held the new title of "rabbi" and exerted their authority over all Jews. They attempted to suppress all of the other sects of Judaism, of which Christianity was thought to be one.

In the course of his duties, Paul was traveling on the road to Damascus. Along the road Paul was overwhelmed by a vision of the risen Christ. The Christ spoke to him and said to him, "Why do you persecute me? Believe in me!". Paul instantly became a devout Christian believer. He went into synagogues to preach Christianity. When he did not get a welcoming reception in the synagogues, he began to go to Gentile communities. There he found success for his message. Paul came into conflict with the early Jewish Christian Church, led by James the brother of Jesus. Paul soon became the leader of the growing Christian Church. The Jewish Church, centered in Jerusalem, fell silent.

In the time of Paul, early Christian communities were growing in areas around the eastern Roman Empire. Paul visited many of these communities to spread the message and to teach proper Christian belief and behavior. Paul wrote letters to Christian communities answering their questions. These letters, the Epistles of Paul, make up the bulk of the Christian New Testament. Modern Christian historical scholars question whether Paul himself actually wrote all of the epistles attributed to him, but this corpus has been accepted in historical Christianity as the words of Paul, and we will treat it as such. In his letters Paul develops the doctrine of the Christ

27

and explains how a Christian ought to live. In Paul's time the first Christian believers were dying. This created a crisis in the life of the Church. Jesus would not return to Earth in time to save all Christians from death. Paul explained how Christianity was a religion for the long term, even if the Second Coming of Christ was not immanent.

The public life and career of Paul is told in the New Testament Book of Acts. The new religion of Christianity, once it was no longer a sect of Judaism, was not a legally recognized religion in the Roman Empire. Innovation in matters of religion was not acceptable in the eyes of the Empire, and Paul fell into trouble with the law. He received hearings before both Jewish and Roman authorities. Before the Jewish authorities Paul claimed to be a true Jew, a Pharisee and a descendant of the Tribe of Benjamin.

This claim is confusing to Jewish readers. Tribal identity had ceased amongst Jews in the time of Kings David and Saul, over a thousand years earlier. Jews are often puzzled when Christian friends ask them to which tribe they belong. One reason for this question is that Christians read the Jewish Bible, the Old Testament, and may not realize that Jews have evolved over the succeeding three thousand years. Another reason is that Paul offers a tribal identity, which suggests that Jews still belonged to tribes in the First Century. We have no idea what Paul meant. We also do not know what it means that he identified as a Pharisee. The Pharisees are mentioned often in Jewish sources and in the New Testament, but no individual names are associated with them. The only two people in recorded history to identity as a Pharisee are Paul, the founder of Gentile Christianity, and Josephus, from the same period, a Jewish general who went over to the Romans during the Great Jewish Rebellion of 66-70 and tried to promote mutual understanding between Romans and Jews. What could the self-

28

identification of Paul and Josephus as Pharisees possibly have meant?

We do not understand exactly what happened during Paul's trials, but it seems that eventually he was sent to Rome where he was executed by the Empire. Paul was one of a growing number of Christian martyrs who were killed for being Christian until the Roman Emperor Constantine made Christianity legal in the Fourth Century.

Paul's doctrine of the Christ is immensely important not only for Christian faith, but also for Christian-Jewish relations. Although Paul created Gentile Christianity, he seemed to believe that Jews in the Church would remain Jews. There is no indication that Paul ceased to observe Jewish law, only that he allowed Gentile Christians not to observe it. Paul said that the Jewish people remain God's covenant people, as stated in the Hebrew Bible, while Christians by their faith join that covenant as "a wild branch grafted onto the olive tree", in Paul's own words. (Romans 11)

On the other hand, Paul explained Christianity largely by contrasting it to Judaism. Paul describes Christianity and Judaism as an either-or. Had Judaism worked, Christianity would not be necessary. Jesus had to come as the Christ because Judaism failed to bring salvation to the world, or even to Jews. Paul contrasts faith, the Christian way, to works (deeds, mitzvot), the Jewish way. Paul says that there is no salvation through works, but only through faith.

Paul's teaching of salvation through faith is not only the opposite of Jewish teaching, it is also controversial within Christianity. As the Christian Church became the religion of nations and empires, it became necessary for Christians to develop Christian laws and behavioral expectations. Certain Protestant groups object to this development and attempt to return to a more purely Pauline position of salvation through faith alone. The debate over how strictly to follow Paul in this matter is a source of division amongst Christians. Paul's teaching of salvation through faith in Christ is essential to Christianity and is a point of departure from Judaism.

# CHAPTER FIVE: THE CHRISTIAN BIBLE AND THE JEWISH BIBLE

## THE NEW TESTAMENT AND THE TALMUD

### One Bible, Two Religions

We have seen that the relationship between Judaism and Christianity is complicated by the way Paul explains the then-new religion of Christianity by contrasting it to the already well-established religion of Judaism. Paul's use of Judaism to explain Christianity ties Judaism and Christianity to one another in an intimate relationship that is shared by few other religions. Judaism and Christianity are even more deeply tied to one another by the fact that they share a common Holy Scriptures. These are the books that Jews call the Bible (TaNaKh, Hebrew Bible, Torah Prophets and Writings) and which Christians call the Old Testament.

The playwright George Bernard Shaw once said the British and the Americans are two nations, divided by a common language. That witticism could be even more appropriately applied to Judaism and Christianity. Jews and Christians have a common set of holy books which they read and interpret differently, leading to many misunderstandings. These misunderstandings are not despite sharing a holy book but because of sharing a holy book.

Most religions are not able to engage in interfaith debate. This is because debate requires a common premise, and few religions share a common premise. Each religion is based upon its own truth claims, which are not relevant to the truth claims of any other religion. For example, each religion may claim certain miracles in relation to its founder, which other religions simply deny. Each religion may claim that its holy book comes from God, which again other religions simply deny.

In the case of the Hebrew Bible, Jews and Christians both claim that this book is the Word of God, however "Word of God" is understood. Jews and Christians are enabled by this common belief to have a lively and often contentious debate over the meaning of the Word.

The concept of the Messiah, a future King of the Jews, developed in Judaism shortly before the rise of Christianity. We will explore the evolution of this idea in a later chapter. This idea, as it gained force, was rooted in the interpretation of certain verses in the Bible. We may call these the Messianic Verses. In the early development of Christianity and Rabbinic Judaism both religions accepted the same set of verses, mostly from the prophet Isaiah, as a reference to the Messiah – either the Jewish future king, or the Christian Christ. The proper understanding of these verses gave Christians and Jews a basis for interfaith debate, with each side claiming the proper understanding of what both sides agreed is God's Word.

In the past two centuries this mode of debate has diminished as historical study has revealed the gap of centuries between the original intention of the prophets and the messianic interpretation. Conversionary arguments based on the Messianic Verses are still common amongst Christian Fundamentalists who believe that the Christian messianic understanding is the original intention of the Prophets.

**The Hebrew Bible**

The Hebrew Bible consists of approximate twenty-four books (depending on how one divides them one from another) separated into three sections.

The first section of the Hebrew Bible is the five books of the Torah – Genesis, Exodus, Leviticus, Numbers and Deuteronomy. These books contain 11 chapters which tell the ancient Jews' understanding of creation and human prehistory. The rest tells the early story of the Jewish people, from

Abraham and Sarah through the death of Moses, focusing on the liberation of Israelite slaves from Egypt and their forty years of wandering in the desert before their entry into the promised land. The Torah contains a number of law codes which are the basis for the 613 commandments of Judaism. A central principle of Judaism is that Jewish practice and faith are based only in the Torah, the first five books of the Bible. The rest of the books are only for inspiration.

The second section of the Hebrew Bible is the books of the Prophets. The first half of the Prophets section tells the history of the Jews from the entry into the Promised Land, through the rise of the kings Saul, David, Solomon and their successors, through the Babylonian conquest and destruction of Judah and Jerusalem in 586 BCE and the immediate aftermath of the destruction. The second half of the Prophets contains the written words of certain prophets of God. There are three long books of Isaiah, Jeremiah and Ezekiel and one book of the shorter books of twelve other prophets.

The third section of the Hebrew Bible is the Writings, containing ancient Hebrew literature including Psalms, Proverbs, Job, some shorter works, and some historical books which describe the return from Babylonian Exile around the year 500 BCE.

The three sections of the Hebrew Bible were established and sanctified at different times. The Torah was declared holy at the time of the return from Babylon. The books of the Prophets were sanctified over a period of time in the early days of the Second Jewish Temple of Jerusalem, through a process unknown to us. By the time of Jesus, the section of the Prophets was established and closed. Thus, the Holy Bible known to Jesus consisted of two sections, the Torah and the Prophets. In early Christian writing the Torah is often called the Law, as the Greek term for Torah is Nomos which means "law." The word Torah actually means "teaching" or "guidance" according to its Hebrew root. Jesus called his Bible "the Torah and the Prophets" – in Greek translation, "the Law and the Prophets."

The third section of the Hebrew Bible, the Writings, contains books which were in existence at the time of Jesus but had not yet been added into the Bible. The collection of the Writings was established and closed after the Roman destruction of the Second Jerusalem Temple in the year 70. The "rabbis", the newly appointed leaders of the Jewish people after the destruction, closed the Jewish Bible forever when they voted which books to include in the Writings and which to exclude.

In traditional Rabbinic Judaism the three sections of the Hebrew Bible are in descending order of holiness. The Torah is believed to be the spoken word of God, given to Moses at Mount Sinai at the beginning of Jewish history. The Prophets spoke in the Spirit of Prophecy, through the visions of the prophets. The message is from God, but the words are the words of the prophets themselves. The Writings are given in the Holy Spirit, which in Judaism means something like "divine inspiration." The authors of the Writings are authors in the modern sense, but a divine spirit guided their endeavors. For example, Psalm 23, which is attributed to King David, was believed to be written by him based on his personal experience as a shepherd.

To Christians, the threefold division of the Hebrew Bible has no meaning. It is all the Old Testament. Christians tend to grant the greatest level of holiness to Isaiah and certain other prophetic books, and the Book of Daniel which Jews place in the Writings but which Christians often place in the Prophets, because these books are the basis for the Messianic Verses.

Christians added a fourth section to the Old Testament, the Apocrypha. These are books which the Rabbis after the year 70 rejected from the Writings, but which early Christians considered holy. These books are preserved in the Greek language, but most were originally composed in Hebrew or Aramaic. Protestants do not include the Apocrypha in the Old Testament.

The Bible was closed by the early Rabbis at the same time, just after the destruction of the Second Jerusalem Temple, that Christianity and Rabbinic Judaism were forming out of the elements of early Judaism. As Christianity and the rabbinic form of Judaism (which is the only Judaism familiar to us) came into being, each religion published new holy books which they granted authority equal to the Hebrew Bible. For Christians this new set of holy books is the New Testament. For Jews it is the Mishnah and, some centuries later, the Talmud, which is based upon the Mishnah.

**The New Testament**

The New Testament, like the Hebrew Bible, has different sections, all composed at about the same time in the earliest years of Christianity.

The first section is the Four Gospels – Matthew, Mark, Luke and John, named for their reputed authors. Each of the Gospels teaches Christianity through the vehicle of biography, telling the life story of Jesus. Matthew and Luke tell the birth story which is well known from Christmas, but the central concern of the Gospels is the story of the arrest, trial and death of Jesus on a cross. This part of the story is called the Passion. Although the Gospels tell the story of Jesus in chronological order, their central interest is in reverse order. Placed before the Passion narrative are stories of Jesus' one or two years of public preaching, from his immersion in the Jordan River by John the Baptist up to his final meal with his closest disciples. This meal was possibly an early version of a Passover seder.

The first three Gospels tell the story of Jesus in similar, almost parallel ways. For this reason they are called the Synoptic Gospels. Synopsis means that they can be easily matched one to another, though there are significant differences in detail. The three Synoptic Gospels paint Jesus as a preacher who demanded radical life changes from his followers in anticipation of the immanent coming of the Kingdom of God. He preached a demanding ethical code while expressing disdain for some of the ritual fashions of the day and for outward displays of piety. Jesus in the Synoptic Gospels is not aware of the ultimate "Christian" meaning of his existence until the very end, perhaps just as he is dying on the cross.

John, the fourth Gospel, portrays Jesus differently. The Jesus of John is aware from the beginning of his mission that he is the Christ, God become human. John gives a different chronology for Jesus' activities. In the Gospel of John, Jesus dies on the eve of Passover, at the time of the sacrifice of the Paschal lamb, so Jesus' last supper is not a Passover observance.

The differences between the four Gospels may be in part because of different early Christian remembrances of Jesus' life, but they are more directly due to the different views of the Gospel writers on Christian doctrine. Biography in Roman times was only secondarily a way of recording the facts of a human life; it was primarily a way of teaching lessons on how one ought to live.

The word Gospel means "good news." The good news for Christians is that their Savior died on the cross to save them from the consequences of human sinfulness. The life story of Jesus is a way of sharing this message. In the past two centuries, as ethical living in this world has taken on a more important role in the way people view religion, the ethical aspects of Jesus' teaching have received renewed emphasis, in particular the obligation to love one another. In historical

Christianity this element, though present, was secondary to the question of the meaning of Jesus' death on the cross for Christian believers.

The next part of the New Testament is the Book of Acts, which tells the history of the early Christian Church. The Book of Acts focuses on Peter, who organized the Christian Church and is seen as the first Pope, and Paul, who established Gentile Christianity and developed the central doctrines of Christianity. The Book of Acts records the conflict between James, the brother of Jesus, who believed that Christianity was just for Jews, and Paul, who triumphed with his teaching that Christianity was for all nations. The Book of Acts teaches that a Christian does not have to observe the kosher laws to be a faithful Christian. This was a major step in the evolution of Christianity, for there were many persons in the Roman Empire who admired the Jewish worship of one God but who did not wish to refrain from eating pork and shellfish. The Book of Acts records that Paul was arrested and tried by a Jewish court, after which he was sent to Rome, where presumably he was executed by the Romans for teaching a new and not legal religion.

The next section of the New Testament is the largest. It is the Epistles, or letters, primarily the letters of Paul. As Paul traveled from place to place promoting the new religion of Christianity he was recognized as the ultimate authority by young Christian communities that were forming throughout the Roman Empire. These communities wrote to Paul with their urgent questions about how to live as Christians and what a Christian must believe. Paul's letters in response to these requests constitute the earliest formulation of Christian doctrine. Although Paul's letters are placed after the Gospels in the Christian New Testament, they are the earliest Christian teachings that we have in written form. The Epistle to the Romans and the Epistle to the Hebrews are especially

37

important in Christian-Jewish relations, as they define the relationship of the new religion to the old, and the relationship of the Christian Community to the Jewish people. We shall return to some of the themes discussed in these letters.

The final book of the New Testament is the Apocalypse of John. This is a different John than the author of the Gospel of John. Apocalypse was a common form of literature in late Second Temple Judaism. Typical of apocalyptic writing is the belief that God is about to bring the universe as we know it to an end. God will change all the laws of nature and bring about a new world where righteousness will be triumphant, evildoers will be punished, and good people will be rewarded. This transformation is soon to occur, and will be introduced by a time of war and great troubles in the world. Jesus was himself an apocalyptic preacher. The earliest Christians expected Jesus to return soon to earth to bring about the end time. As this end time did not come quickly, Christians transformed their expectations for a long wait. The Apocalypse of John may have been inspired by the Roman destruction of the Temple in the year 70, or by the eruption of Mount Vesuvius in the year 79. These events may have made it seem that the end time was immanent. Historical scholars debate whether the Apocalypse of John originates in Christian or Jewish circles. I believe that the book in its current form is a Christian rewrite of an earlier Jewish apocalyptic work.

For Jews and Christians to understand one another we must realize that the most notable event in First Century Judaism was not the death of Jesus on the cross, which was barely noticed at the time except by Jesus' closest inner circle of followers, but the destruction of the Holy Temple in Jerusalem at the end of the Great Jewish Rebellion of 66-70. This event resounded throughout the Roman and Persian Empires, every place where there were Jews, and Gentiles who knew Jews. Although Jesus' crucifixion occurred some 35 years before the destruction of the Temple, after the destruction (*Hurban* in Hebrew), the death of Jesus was interpreted in light of that event. Christianity and Rabbinic Judaism are two different answer to the question, "Why did God allow God's own home on Earth to be destroyed?" The Christian answer is that Jesus, as the ultimate sacrifice, made the animal sacrifices of ancient Judaism unnecessary. Jews did not find this answer compelling but many Gentiles did. The answer of the early Rabbis is that God has punished the Jews for our sins but in the meantime a life of fulfillment of mitzvot (God's commandments) and study of the Torah provides forgiveness of sin and, in due time, a Jewish restoration. The Rabbis taught that the study of sacrificial portions in the Torah, and the observance of mitzvot, is the ultimate sacrifice, while Christianity taught that the death of Jesus on the cross, accessed by the worshiper through faith in Jesus as the Christ, accomplishes all that was formerly accomplished through the Temple service.

**The New Testament and the Talmud**

At the same time that Christians were writing the New Testament the rabbis were composing a book of their own which, like the New Testament, effectively supplanted the Hebrew Bible by providing a new understanding of God's plan for human life on earth. The earliest term for this new Scriptural work is the Oral Torah. The traditions handed down from generation to generation by scholars constitutes the Oral Torah, parallel to the written words in the Bible which are the Written Torah. The Written and Oral Torah together constitute the totality of divine revelation.

The Oral Torah, as its name implies, could not be written down. It had to be taught from teacher to student. Eventually the Oral Torah became too large to be memorized. The old prohibition was overruled. Around the year 200 Rabbi Judah the Prince, ruler of the Jews in the region of Judea and head of the Sanhedrin, authorized the publication of the Mishnah, a compendium of teachings of the Oral Torah. Further explication and writing of the teachings of the Oral Torah led to the publication of the Jerusalem Talmud (actually created in the Galilee) around the year 400 and the Babylonian Talmud around the year 700. The Babylonian Talmud is the ultimate authority for how to live by the Bible. If a Jew wishes to know the proper way to live by the commandments of the Torah reference must be made to the Talmud, not the written Bible itself. Jewish institutions such as the synagogue, the schoolhouse, the law court and the academy of higher studies (yeshivah) are known not from the written Bible but from the Talmud. Established Jewish practices such as thrice daily prayer, the liturgy, the Passover seder, Hannukah candles, and Yom Kippur soul-searching are all found not in the written Bible but in the Talmud.

In the Talmud, the often fierce deity of the ancient Israelites has become known as the gentle, compassionate and loving God of the Jews.

In the Talmud, the *lex talionis*, the commandment of "eye for an eye" receives its proper interpretation as the equality of all persons before the law, regardless of social or economic status. It is not a law of vengeance. The monetary value of an eye is determined by the courts, as in American law.

**Comparing the Christian and Jewish Scriptures**

The term "Old Testament" is judgmental. It means old and rejected, old and replaced by the superior New Testament. Many contemporary Christians show respect to Judaism by using instead of Old Testament the term Hebrew Bible. This identifies the Jewish Scriptures by their language of composition, while the New Testament is composed in the Greek language.

40

Many modern-day people attempt to compare Christianity to Judaism by comparing the Old Testament to the New Testament. Readers of this book may even have been expecting such a comparison. A comparison of the New Testament to the Old Testament (Hebrew Bible) is inherently invalid because it compares a text from the Roman period to a text from the Ancient Near East. The books of the Hebrew Bible were written hundreds, even a thousand years before the books of the New Testament. The comparison of the New Testament to the Old Testament is also unfortunate because it has been used all too often for the purpose of demonstrating the ethical and spiritual superiority of Christianity to Judaism. Especially in the modern era, when ethics is often thought of as the central purpose of religion, the most ethically refined texts in the New Testament have been invidiously compared to some of the most ethically problematic texts in the Hebrew Bible.

The Jewish people evolved gradually from a group of warlike Early Iron Age tribespeople who fought desperately to maintain their territory in an era of vast human movements across the globe. The nations of Israel and Judah struggled to maintain their integrity in the face of the Assyrian Empire, who ruled with tremendous cruelty and disregard for human life. Many of the ethically troubling texts in the Old Testament, such as the list of curses in Deuteronomy 28 and descriptions of great massacres, reflect the horrifying life experience of victims of the Assyrian conquests. Gradually, after the experience of conquest and exile, the people of the Kingdom of Judah evolved into the Jewish people. The Jewish ethical teachings of the New Testament reflect a thousand years of Jewish evolution.

If you are reading this book, we may presume you desire harmonious relations between Christians and Jews and a positive appreciation of each religion by the other. That being the case, we should compare the ethical teachings of each religion by comparing the best of the New Testament to the best of the Mishnah and Talmud. We recognize that each religion has its roots in the Hebrew Bible, while the trunk and branches develop in different ways. There should be no more invidious comparisons between harsh Old Testament justice and New Testament grace. Let us rather listen closely and hear what each religion says of itself when it is putting forward its highest angels. Unfortunately, many American Jews know their own religion primarily from unflattering stereotypes that are common in our culture. Just as we ask of our neighbors, we must learn to appreciate our religion for what it says of itself, based in the sacred literature.

## The Oral Torah of the Rabbis: Mishnah and Talmud

The Oral Torah of rabbinic Judaism defies easy description. Unlike the Hebrew Bible and the New Testament, it is not written in the form of books and letters, history and biography etc., genres of written literature which are familiar to us. The Mishnah is written in the form of a collection of rabbinic opinions on various topics of Jewish law. While the Hebrew Bible raises issues of practice and divine service haphazardly, the Mishnah organizes Jewish law into six major headings – the six books of the Mishnah – subdivided into sixty subheadings called tractates. The law is not presented in the Mishnah. Rather, the Mishnah collects the contrasting legal opinions of the great sages of Roman-era Judaism, without deciding between them. The Talmud contains the opinions of later Sages on the legal opinions of the earlier Sages. The Talmud presents these literary discussions as if they were actual discussions between the various Sages, most likely reproducing the type of debate that took place in the rabbinic academies of learning. The Mishnah is about the same size as the Hebrew Bible, but the Talmud is much longer. All told, a volume of the Talmud would fill a three-foot bookshelf with large folio sized books. About a third of the material in the

Talmud is not legal in nature. There are stories about the Sages, proverbs, folklore, and other genres of literature. It is all disjointed, with one piece not following another in any predictable way. The Talmud cannot be read, only studied. Thus, the oral nature of the written material is newly expressed each time one opens the Talmud. As the Talmud contains the teachings of hundreds of Sages, spanning centuries, some living in the Land of Israel and others in Babylon, one can never say with authority "the Talmud says ....". One can only quote teachings and opinions of varying authority that are found in the Talmud.

There is one section of the Mishnah, the Sayings of the Fathers (*Pirkei Avot*) which contains the ethical and wisdom sayings of the early Sages about how one may live a righteous life. The Pirkei Avot has always been popular with the Jewish masses. With some justice it has been called the Jewish Sermon on the Mount, in that the Sermon on the Mount (Matthew 5-7) collects ethical teachings attributed to Jesus.

**The Bible and the Importance of the Jews to Christianity**

Jews are often amazed at how important we are to Christians. Whether we are loved or reviled, we Jews are the subject of a lot of Christian attention. This is rare in the history of religions. One cannot readily discover any other instance of a religion which is so concerned with another religion.

Many Jews presume that Jews are so important to Christianity because Jesus was a Jew. This is certainly a factor, but not as important as many Jews would believe. The modern focus on history has made Christians acutely aware of the Jewish circumstances of Jesus' life, but through most of history the average Christian naturally thought of Jesus as a Christian.

The Jews are also important to Christianity because Paul makes so much reference to Judaism in explaining his own religion. Paul teaches the new doctrines of Christianity by contrasting them to the older and better known religion of Judaism. Most Jews are not all that familiar with the Epistles of Paul, so that would not explain to Jews why we are so important to Christians.

The Jews are important to Christianity because the authors of the Gospels and other books of the New Testament make frequent reference to the Hebrew Bible. There are quotes from the Bible, especially in the Gospel of Matthew, and the story of Jesus' life and Passion is told in such a way as to remind a person who was familiar with the Hebrew Bible of certain passages. Because the New Testament echoes many passages in the Hebrew Bible, many Christians believe that the Hebrew Bible exists to predict and lead up to Jesus and the Christian religion. To Jews, this echoing is a demonstration that the authors of the New Testament books knew and revered the Hebrew Bible and used it as a pattern for their own writing. Jews do not see the Hebrew Bible as a prediction of Jesus, any more than a person writing about last week's snowstorm is predicting the weather. This distinction is obscured by the fact that traditional Jews also saw the Bible as predicting the future – the Jewish future. Modern historical analysis makes it easy for Christians and Jews to distinguish the original intent of the Prophets of the Hebrew Bible from the way their words were understood later in Judaism and Christianity, but pre-modern people did not have these tools of historical analysis available to them.

While the New Testament often refers to the Hebrew Bible, it would be possible for the New Testament to exist on its own as the sole Christian Scriptures. There were some early Christians who argued that this should be the case. But Christians chose to preserve the entire Hebrew Bible as part of their own Scriptures. The full Christian word of God consists of the Jewish Bible plus the New Testament. This is the most significant reason that the Jews are so important to Christians.

Not because Jesus was Jewish, but because Christians revere the Hebrew Bible as sacred Scriptures, and that Hebrew Bible is all about – us, the Jews.

Muslims recognize the Hebrew Bible and the New Testament as divine revelations, but they do not regularly study these texts. Christians study the Hebrew Bible along with the New Testament. This creates a relationship between Judaism and Christianity not found between any other two major religions. When Christians read the Hebrew Bible they do not find within it what Jews find within it. Most Christians read the Hebrew Bible as a forerunner and predictor of the New Testament. The words are the same but Christians and Jews hear them differently. This can be difficult for people of both religions to understand.

There is nothing unusual in any tribe, people or nation believing that it has a special mission. That is probably true about just about any nation, including the mixture of many peoples that makes up the American nation. What is unusual about the Jews is that because Christians and also Muslims accept that the Hebrew Bible is the Word of God, they also recognize the Jews as God's Chosen People. It makes life complicated for us Jews. It has not always been beneficial to us to be perceived as God's Chosen People, though it is certainly an honor. In most times and places, Chosen People has meant to Jews, chosen for the honorable responsibility of being a holy people and bearing witness to God. It should not be understood as a superiority claim, especially as the Hebrew Bible emphasizes that all human beings are equally created in God's image. Admittedly, in times of persecution, Jews have consoled ourselves with grand ideas about our significance in God's plan. It is ironic that non-Jewish fringe religious groups who identify themselves as the "real" Israelites often take the concept of the Chosen People as evidence that members of their group are naturally superior to other human beings. Jews take no responsibility for such claims. American Jews are often self-conscious and embarrassed about the concept of the Chosen People. I was one of those Jews, until a devout Christian friend told me to accept who I am and live up to it.

When the Christian Church became fully organized after the Roman Empire adopted the Christian religion in the Fourth Century, the Roman rulers established the acceptable form of Christianity. Other forms of Christianity which deviated from the norm were suppressed as heresy, false belief. The Church at that time could have decided that Judaism is not a separate and distinct religion but a heresy of Christianity. Had that decision been made, and it was considered, then Judaism would have been ruthlessly suppressed. The Church decided instead to recognize the Jews as the people of the Bible. The Jews have a covenant relationship with God, said the Church, and that relationship is still valid even if it has been replaced by the "superior" covenant of Christianity initiated by Jesus' death on the cross. On this account the lives of Jews must be protected, and Jews may not be forcibly converted. At the same time Jews are to be held in low esteem by society and strongly pressured to convert. The Jews were not treated as equals in the Christian world, but we fared much better than Christian heretics. Jewish survival into the modern age is in large part due to Christian acknowledgment that Jews are the biblical people of God. There were occasions through history of forced conversions and massacres of Jews, but this was contrary to Christian law. When Jewish lives were endangered, Jews often appealed to the Church authorities, who protected them. In modern times Jews expect to be treated as citizens, equal to others regardless of religion. In the premodern world where religious deviance was not accepted, the Jews held a unique right to live by our own laws and practice our own faith. This made the Jews the archetypal minority group in the Christian world. This unique status led to the opening up of the "Jewish Question" (Is there a place for Jews in a modern society?) after the French Revolution.

# CHAPTER SIX: CHRIST, MESSIAH, TORAH –

## Paths to Salvation in Christianity and Judaism

### Salvation

The religious terms "salvation" and "redemption" mean roughly the same thing. Salvation has two different meanings, relating to the individual person or the nation as a whole. Salvation can mean that the individual is excused from whatever divine judgment and punishment awaits so that the soul may go to heaven after mortal death. This is the most usual meaning in Christianity. Salvation can also mean that the nation or people as a whole is saved from calamity, such as enslavement, conquest, disease, oppression, famine and the like. This is the most usual meaning in Judaism. Jews also have a concept of individual salvation, which we shall discuss in our chapter on the afterlife, but the focus of theJewish concept of salvation is more on a better life for the Jewish people in this world.

For Christians, salvation means primarily that through faith in Jesus Christ as the risen Lord one is granted a reprieve from the consequences of human sinfulness and is granted a heavenly reward upon death. Salvation for a Christian is not something earned or achieved, but a gift freely given by a gracious God.

For Jews, salvation means that at the beginning of our history we were slaves in Egypt. God set us free, gave us the Torah, and brought us into the Promised Land of Israel. At the end of time God will gather in all Jewish exiles, restore Jewish sovereignty in our land, and rule over us with justice through a divinely appointed king. In the meantime, our role is to learn and live by the Torah and endure the sufferings of this world until God decides the time of redemption has come.

Both Christians and Jews have, since the Enlightenment, taken a more active view of the human role in bringing God's justice into human society.

## Christ

Jesus is important to Christians not for who he was – Jesus of Nazareth, a Galilean Jew – but for what he was as Christians believe – the Christ. Christianity begins not with the birth of Jesus, nor yet with the Crucifixion, but with the Resurrection. As the Christ, Jesus provides a path to salvation of soul for the Christian believer. The doctrine of the Christ is profound. There is a whole realm of Christian thought, called Christology, to explain the meaning of the Christ. Books on this topic could easily fill a whole library. What we present here is the barest outline.

God chooses to become human with one aspect of God's being, an aspect which is called the Son. God does this by causing a virgin woman to become pregnant and give birth. The child who is born, named Jesus, is both human and divine. This process is called the Incarnation.

Jesus fulfills his divine mission on earth by dying. He is crucified, suffers and dies. Jesus' death is an atonement sacrifice for humankind. Jesus' death represents not just a human sacrifice; it is God's own self that is sacrificed. Once this mission is accomplished the Son returns to his heavenly source beside the Father, who is another aspect of God. Jesus' rise from the grave and return to heaven is called the Resurrection. The Holy Spirit, the third aspect of God, descends to earth to guide the Christian community, the Church.

The Father, the Son and the Holy Spirit constitute the Christian Holy Trinity.

The atonement accomplished through Jesus' sacrifice is available to all human beings on condition that they believe that Jesus is the Christ. Those who do not believe are not redeemed and are not forgiven for their sins. Those who do believe are "saved." Their souls are purified through their faith and may go to a heavenly reward after death.

Since only believers are saved, it is important for Christians to believe correctly and to express that belief properly in their life and worship. One difference between Catholics and Protestants is the way they invoke God in their benedictions. Catholic Christians pray in the name of the Father, the Son and the Holy Spirit. Protestants pray in the name of Jesus. They claim that Catholic prayers will not be heard because the name of Jesus must be spoken. Of course, Jews have no stake in this debate. Jews invoke and bless only in the name of God. A Jew should not say "amen" to a prayer spoken in the name of either Jesus or the Father, the Son and the Holy Spirit. To do so would constitute a statement of Christian faith, which would make light of true Christian faith and would deny the principles of Judaism.

The doctrine of the Christ is succinctly expressed in a verse from the Gospel of John:

For God so loved the world, that he gave his only begotten Son, that whosoever believes in him shall not perish, but have everlasting life. (John 3:16).

This is the most quoted biblical verse in the Christian world. One might see a fan holding up a sign that says "John 3:16" behind the goalposts at a football game. Many Christians publicize this verse as much as possible in order to spread belief in the Christ.

Jews are often skeptical of the claims of Christian faith. Do Christians really believe in the virgin birth and the Incarnation? Do they really believe that our Jewish brother who was

50

executed over two thousand years ago by the Romans is God become human? What does the average American of today believe about the virgin birth, the Incarnation, the Resurrection, and the atoning sacrifice of Jesus as the Son of God? Many Americans of today had very little religious upbringing and do not think about it much. Of those who are observant Christians, I have observed that many fall into three different groups. There are those who believe that all happened as described, and anyone who denies the reality of these events is denying the basis of Christianity. There are those who do not take the events literally but believe that they are philosophically true. Many professors of religion of my acquaintance take this point of view. This was also the view of many of America's Founding Fathers. A third point of view is that of cultural Christians, who take no stand on the validity of faith statements but believe that Christendom is a great world civilization which has generated timeless values. I have also met many faithful American Christians who do not fit into any of these three general categories. Religion and faith are not easily reduced to simple motivations or rational explanations. As Jews we stand outside all of these categories, but we are deeply affected by them. Our view of our own religion and our way of living it or rejecting it is much influenced by the beliefs and attitudes of our neighbors. There are many Christians who do not think too much about the scientific and logical challenges to traditional Christian beliefs. They have a strong personal relationship with Jesus. They feel loved. They rejoice in the sensation of being saved. "I was lost, and now I am found," in the words of the Christian hymn *Amazing Grace*. The abstract God of Judaism and Islam can seem a little distant. The mental picture of God as a fellow human, suffering more than you have ever suffered and all for your sake, is a powerfully attractive image. Even a Jew who is confirmed and fully comfortable within Judaism can understand and admire the attraction of the Christ idea.

51

## Messiah

Christians use the Hebrew word Messiah as a synonym for the Greek word Christ. Thus, Christians will say that Jesus is the Messiah, by which they mean that Jesus is the Christ. The Messiah has a different meaning in Judaism.

The Jewish Messiah is a future king, descended from the royal line of King David, who will restore Jewish sovereignty in the Land of Israel, establish justice according to the laws of the Torah, and defeat the enemies of the Jewish people so that the Jews are no longer threatened. In some more apocalyptic forms of Judaism the Messiah will defeat all evil on earth, install the reign of God over all humankind, and usher in a thousand-year era of universal peace, righteousness and prosperity.

While the goal of the Christ in Christianity is to provide salvation to believers, the role of the Messiah in Judaism is to bring justice on earth. The Christ saves humankind from sinfulness. In Judaism there is no such thing as sinfulness, only sin, which is a deed not a state of being.

The doctrine of the Messiah evolved gradually in Judaism, and was not yet fully developed in the time of Jesus. The first mention of a messianic future hope in Jewish writing comes from the century before Jesus, in the Psalms of Solomon. To pray for God to send the Messiah in Jesus' time had a very simple meaning – it meant that one was not happy with the current rulers of the Kingdom of Judah. Those who were pleased with the rule of the High Priest, such as the historian Josephus, make no mention of a messiah. Those who were displeased with the rule of the High Priest, such as the Dead Sea Scrolls community, prayed for a messiah.

King David ruled over the combined kingdom of Judah and Israel around the year 1,000 BCE. He established Jerusalem as his capital and initiated the construction of the Holy Temple which was completed during the reign of David's son

Solomon. The dynasty of King David lasted 500 years, an unusually long run for any royal house. The High Priest in David's time, Zadok, established a high priestly dynasty which lasted even longer, until the time of the Maccabees.

The last Davidic king of Judah was Zerubabbel, in early Persian Empire times. In circumstances unknown to us, but probably because of a rebellion, Zerubbabel was removed from his throne. That is the last we ever hear from the line of King David. During the centuries of the Second Temple, the Jews were ruled by a Zadokite High Priest. Josephus praises this form of government as "the rule of God, the most excellent form of government." After the events of Hannukah the Zadokite high priests were overthrown by the Hasmonean family of priests from the village of Modi'in. Many Jews did not accept the Hasmoneans as legitimate. The Hasmoneans created further outrage when they usurped the throne of the kingdom, calling themselves King as well as High Priest. A few decades before the birth of Jesus, the outrage was inflamed when the Romans appointed Herod as king over Judah. Herod was Jewish but he was an Idumean, not a Judean, so Herod did not fulfill the Torah's requirement that the king be native born (The US Constitution has a similar requirement.) The Romans appointed and removed high priests at will out of a pool of priestly families. Jews who were unhappy with this arrangement longed for the Messiah – which is to say, a true King of Judah.

The early rabbis who ruled after the destruction of the Temple in the year 70 attempted to suppress messianic yearnings, not because of internal government issues which had become moot after the destruction, but because messianism had led to self-destructive rebelliousness against the mighty Roman Empire. The first rabbinic leader, Rabbi Yohanan ben Zakkai, said: If you are planting a tree and you hear that the messiah has come, finish planting the tree. (Avot d'Rabbi Natan 31) A generation later Rabbi Akiva declared Simeon bar Kochba, leader of a new rebellion against Rome, to be the Messiah. The bar Kochba rebellion (132-35 CE) led to the death of a multitude of Jews, including Rabbi Akiva himself and many of the rabbinic Sages.

The concept of the Messiah evolved in Rabbinic Judaism, as messianic movements came and went. The full-blown apocalyptic myth of the Messiah will be described in a later chapter about the end times. Over the centuries many false messiahs arose to entice the Jews. In 1665 Shabbetai Zevi gained the following of multitudes of the world's Jews. His arrest by the Turkish Sultan and conversion to Islam to save his own life disappointed them all. The Hasidic movement of Judaism arose partially in response to the failure of Shabbetai Zevi. Many Hasidic Jews continue to this day to fervently hope that God will soon send the Messiah. Some Lubavitcher Hasidic Jews believe that their last leader, Rebbe Menachem Mendel Schneerson, is the Messiah. This belief has survived Schneerson's death, a phenomenon that parallels in some ways the faith of the earliest Christians.

The great Medieval rabbi Moses Maimonides took a dim view of the more apocalyptic and fervent messianic hopes of some Jews. In his code of law, *Mishnah Torah*, Maimonides set down the requirements for a Jewish messiah:

The Messianic King will arise in the future and restore the Davidic Kingdom to its former state and original sovereignty. He will build the Temple and gather the dispersed of Israel. All the laws will be re-instituted in his days as in ancient times, sacrifices will be offered, and the Sabbatical and Jubilee years will be observed fully as ordained in the Torah. (Kings 11:1)

Do not think that the Messianic King will have to perform signs and wonders and bring about novel things in the world, or resurrect the dead, and other such things. (Kings 11:3)

If a king arises from the House of David who meditates on the Torah and occupies himself with the commandments like his ancestor David, in accordance with the Written and Oral Torah, and he will prevail upon all Israel to walk in the ways of Torah and strengthen the breaches, and he will fight the battles of God, it may be assumed that he is the Messiah. If he succeeds in all this and rebuilds the Temple on its site and gathers the dispersed of Israel then he is definitely the Messiah. He will then correct the entire world to serve God in unity. (Kings 11:4)

Messianic Christians like to say to Jews: "Why can't Yeshua be my Jewish Messiah?" The answer is very simple: Because when Messianics say Messiah they mean "Christ", and when Jews say Messiah they mean the Jewish King of Israel.

In the interest of interfaith unity many American Christians and Jews like to say to one another, "the only difference between us is that we Christians believe the Messiah has already come, while you Jews are still waiting for him. When he comes, or comes back, we will ask him, and all differences will be resolved." This saying is intended to bring Christians and Jews together, but actually it creates misunderstanding. It leaves Christians wondering why Jews are so stubborn that they refuse to accept their Messiah (the Christ) who is already available to them. It leaves Jews wondering why Christians are so unconcerned with justice in the world that they can claim the Messiah has come while oppression and injustice still prevail. This confusion is eliminated when we understand that Christians and Jews use the word Messiah to mean different things.

**Torah**

Jews believe that Torah is the path to salvation. Not that Jews talk about "salvation" as Christians do, but Jews believe that through study of the Torah and obedience to the

57

commandments of the Torah a person can purify the soul and be righteous in the eyes of God.

For Jews the Messiah has nothing to do with the path of the individual soul to whatever heavenly reward awaits; that is the role of Torah.

We must understand what Jews mean when Jews say the word Torah. In the most literal and limited sense Torah refers to the first five books of the Hebrew Bible – Genesis, Exodus, Leviticus, Numbers, Deuteronomy. Jews do not often use the word "Bible". When Jews say "Torah" or "the Written Torah" they often include the rest of the books of the Hebrew Bible in that word.

Torah extends to the rabbinical interpretations of how to interpret and live by the Written Torah. The Talmud and related rabbinic writings are called the "Oral Torah". The entire Torah includes both the Written and Oral Torah. Jewish tradition teaches that the Oral Torah, like the Written Torah, originates with Moses at Mount Sinai.

One rabbinic tradition contrasts Judaism and Christianity in relation to the Oral Torah, recognizing that Christians also revere the Written Torah as Scriptures. God has Moses memorize the Oral Torah on Mount Sinai. Moses says to God, "Why are you telling me all this? Why don't you write it down like the Written Torah?" God responds to Moses: Someday others who are not Jews will claim to have the Torah, and you will say to them, "Do you have the whole Torah? Do you have the Oral Torah?" Then the Jews will know that only they have the whole Torah. This midrash, with its contentious tone, is clearly a response to Christian claims that the New Testament is the completion of the Old Testament. Naturally Jews deny the sanctity of the New Testament and Christians deny the sanctity of the Talmud. Each religion has its own Scriptures. It is fair to contrast Christianity to Judaism by comparing the New Testament to the Talmud.

Jewish mystics include the Zohar, the basic text of Kabbalah, in the Scriptures. They call the Bible "the Written Torah", the Talmud "the Oral Torah", and the Zohar "the hidden Torah." On the one hand Torah is all based on the Revelation at Mount Sinai in the time of Moses. On the other hand Torah is a continuous process of unfolding revelation which generates new sacred writings.

Torah is acquired first and foremost through education. If the first obligation of a Christian is to believe, the first obligation of a Jew is to study. Because Torah is acquired through learning, the Jews established a system of universal education for Jewish boys and adult men. While they were two thousand years ahead of their time, they were not yet able to imagine education for girls. The Jews developed the institution of the heder, or elementary school, for Bible study, the yeshiva, or school of higher education, for the study of the Oral Torah, and the beit midrash, or library/study house, for continuing study by men according to their capacity and educational level. If learning is the path to salvation, there must be a way for each person to achieve that salvation. Consistent with the times, women were perceived as enablers for their menfolk to study, though on rare occasions women were also educated.

In America the most important role of the Bible is as a source of sacred stories. This view of the Bible derives from the Protestant Sunday School model of religious education, which was based on two foundations – catechism, a list of required beliefs, and Bible stories. The American Jewish Sunday School, based on the Protestant model, also represents the Bible as primarily a source of stories. Historically, Jews did not view the Bible as a story book. The significance of Torah in traditional Judaism is that it is the source of the 613 commandments, *mitzvot* in Hebrew. (*mitzvah* in the singular). The mitzvot are the basis for all Jewish behavioral objectives.

In Judaism, faith follows from deeds. In Christianity, deeds follow from faith. The modern psychological theory of cognitive dissonance suggests that people will not live long in a situation where their actions and beliefs are contradictory. Either starting point leads to a similar end, wherein faith and deeds are consistent with one another. A Jew will move from righteous works to faith. A Christian will move from faith to acts of righteousness.

The Greeks translated the word Torah as nomos, "law." In the New Testament the Torah is called "The Law." This gives Christians the somewhat misleading notion that Judaism is based on obedience to a set of laws. This is true, but it misses the sacred meaning that Torah has for Jews. The word Torah more accurately means "guidance, teaching, instruction." If one loves the Ruler, one submits to the decrees of the Ruler. A Jew is supposed to be good not just for goodness' sake, but for the sake of loyal service to God. The mitzvot, the commandments, even though they define human behaviors, also constitute the theology of Judaism. As the ancient Rabbis said, "One knows the Commander from the nature of the commandments." We know that God is loving and compassionate and forgiving because God has commanded us to exhibit these qualities. The specific behavioral obligations of Judaism are called *halacha*. *Halacha* is the collective term for Jewish law and also the term for a specific law. The Hebrew word *halacha* literally means not "law" but "way." Halacha is the Jewish "way." If Christians hear "halacha" as "way" rather than "law" they may come to a more sympathetic understanding of how Jews experience being Jewish. Paul denigrated the law in some respects, but he spoke very positively of the Christian "way." We can with mutual respect state that both Christians and Jews have a "way" which leads us to a good and blessed life and to ultimate salvation. We may wish to recognize that every religion and culture represents a "way" to live rightly as a human.

Modern Jewish movements other than Orthodoxy have departed from law, halacha, as the central defining characteristic of the Jew. One may ask, then, in what way Reform Judaism and other modern movements differ from Paul? It is a challenging question. Modern Jewish religious movements are still mitzvah oriented even if they see mitzvah more as opportunity or spiritual guidance than as a basis for communal laws.

Jews traditionally believe that Torah study and performance of mitzvot does more than guide individual behavior. It transforms and purifies the human soul, generating a righteous person. As a Christian expects faith to purify a Christian person and transform their human nature so as to live a better life, Jews expect Torah study to accomplish this mission. Both religions expect the faithful and observant individual to become a better person, to be gracious in their interactions with others, and to strive for justice in appreciation for God's gifts.

It is misleading to compare Christianity and Judaism by comparing their doctrines of the Messiah. It is sensible to compare and contrast Christianity and Judaism by comparing the Christ to the Torah. This will make both Christians and Jews feel fairly represented. It should be noted by Christians that Jews may be awaiting the Messiah but we Jews are not awaiting the Torah. The Torah is with us. That is why Jews do not feel a longing that could be fulfilled in the Christ, a matter of some wonder to many Christians.

Every religion provides a way to live a holy life and a path to ultimate salvation.

For Christians, this is the Way of Christ.

For Jews, this is the Way of Torah.

# CHAPTER SEVEN: ISRAEL AND JUDAH

The word Israel has a complicated history. The oldest use of Israel is as a name for a tribal confederation that later evolved into two kingdoms. The term also is applied to the territory of those tribes and kingdoms – the Land of Israel. By the First Century, the time of Jesus, Israel was used a poetic name for the Jews, the living descendants of those two kingdoms. Israel was also a name for the territory of the political Kingdom of Judah, known also as the Province of Judea in the Roma Empire.

Christians sometimes think that Jews retain tribal identities. They may even ask a Jewish person "Which tribe are you from?", a question for which Jews have no answer. Part of this confusion comes from the fact that Christians think of Jews as the people of the Old Testament. They might not realize that Jews have continued to evolve for three thousand years since the time of Kings David and Solomon, who broke up the tribal territories to establish national unity in their Kingdom. Part of this confusion comes from the fact that Paul, in claiming his Jewish bona fides at his trial before a Jewish court, claims descent from the Tribe of Benjamin. It is hard to know what Paul means by this statement, recorded in the Book of Acts, since by Paul's time no Jew had a tribal identity.

The northern Israelite kingdom was conquered by the Assyrian Empire in 722 BCE. The inhabitants were scattered through the Empire and replaced by other displaced people who became known as the Samaritans. The southern kingdom of Judah was conquered by Babylon in 586 BCE. Her people were scattered by the Babylonians throughout Mesopotamia but retained their identity. They were subsequently known as Jews. There were no more Israelites.

In Greek times, the priestly family of the Hasmoneans reestablished independence for the Kingdom of Judah. The

Hasmonean kings extended their rule over the territory that the Bible assigns to the twelve tribes of Israel. They converted the Gentile Galileans and the Idumeans (Edomites) in their kingdom to Judaism. They conquered Samaria but did not attempt to convert the Samaritans, as the Samaritan religion was already a form of Judaism. The Hasmonean Kingdom of Judah was incorporated into the expanding Roman Empire as the province of Judea. This was the Judean world of Jesus.

The word Jew in Jesus' time could mean a resident in the small territory of Judah, or it could mean a Jewish subject in the expanded Judean Kingdom of the Hasmoneans, or it could refer to a member of this people wherever they were scattered in the world.

The Romans soon removed the Hasmonean rulers from power and made their own favorite, Herod, King of Judea. The High Priests of the Jerusalem Temple continued as the nominal internal rulers of Jewish affairs. Herod the Great died in 4BCE, most likely just before Jesus was born. The Romans then divided up Herod's kingdom into four parts. The Galilee was given to Herod's son, Antipater (Herod Junior). Jesus, as a Galilean from Nazareth, was a subject of Antipater. The central region of Judea including Jerusalem was placed under direct Roman rule. The Romans appointed prefects (not actually procurators, who held a higher rank) to rule over Judea. The High Priest ruled in Jerusalem while the Roman prefect had his capital in Caesarea on the seacoast. The prefect maintained a palace in Jerusalem for when government business brought him to the city. Pontius Pilate, who presided over the trial and conviction of Jesus, was one such prefect. The historian Josephus says that most of the prefects were corrupt, vicious and incompetent, but none so much as Pontius Pilate. Josephus blames the Roman governors who did not do honor to their Roman masters nor their Jewish subjects for the outbreak of the Jewish Rebellion in 66-70 CE.

64

In the Gospel of John the word Jew sometimes means a member of the Jewish people, and sometimes it means a resident of the region of Judah as opposed to a Galilean. The Judeans thought the Galileans to be rude, while the Galileans thought the Judeans to be cosmopolitan snobs.It was much like the cultural conflict between New Yorkers and West Virginians.

The Israeli-Palestinian conflict of our times impinges on all discussions of the Land of Israel and the Kingdom of Judah. It colors Jewish-Christian relations for good or for ill. In the time of Jesus there was no Palestine nor had there ever been. After the two Jewish rebellions against Rome, in 66-70 CE and 132-135, the Romans had enough of Jewish nationhood. They rebuilt and renamed Jerusalem, calling it Aelia Capitolina. The name Jerusalem was restored only after Christian rule began. The Romans renamed Israel "Palestine", after the long-gone Philistines, and attached the territory as an administrative district to the Province of Syria. The name Palestine was retained for the land under the successive colonial administrations who ruled from Rome, then Constantinople, then Damascus, then Baghdad, then Crusaders, then Egypt, then Istanbul, then London. Through all these empires Palestine was the colonial name for this province. The Arab population did not think of themselves as Palestinians. Palestinian national consciousness came into being as a result of the Arab-Israeli conflict. The land where Jesus walked was the kingdom of Judea or the land of Israel. The land can only be called Palestine after the Romans renamed it in the Third Century.

The young Christian Church adopted the biblical name Israel for itself. The Church called itself Israel of the Spirit, which had superseded in God's plan the old Israel of the Flesh, the Jewish people. For two thousand years the Jewish people chafed at being called the "rejected Israel" while the Christians called themselves the "new Israel." Jews and Christians debated over who had the right to call themselves Israel. It may be for this reason that in 1947 the Jewish Agency named the new sovereign Jewish state "Israel." The deliberations over the naming of the state were kept secret, and no rationale for the name was ever stated. The country could have been named Zion after the Zionist Movement. (Zion is a poetic name for Jerusalem.) Historically it made sense to name the new state Judah, like the ancient Kingdom of Judah/Judea. Judah, as the nation of the Jews. The name Israel includes a theological claim, that the old Israel remains Israel to the present day. When the Catholic Church granted diplomatic recognition to the State of Israel in 1993, they implicitly gave recognition to the view that the Church and the Jews are both Israel, each in their own way. This is a major accomplishment after two thousand years of conflict over the name Israel. In modern times Israel is the name of a nation state for which Jew is the name of its people. The modern word Israeli partially resolves that contradiction.

The word Jew is a national term, referring to a member of the Jewish people, a descendant by birth or naturalization of the ancient people of Judah. The word Jew may also be a religious designation, but to be Jewish by religion one must be a member of the Jewish people. This point is often missed in America, where Jews are American citizens of Jewish religion. Jewish is seen as parallel to Catholic or Protestant or Muslim. While this is true, Jewish is also parallel to Polish or Russian or German or English. Jewish Americans are Americans of Jewish ancestry, whether their ancestors immigrated to America from Poland or Russia or Iraq or any other country. The designation Jew refers back to the original homeland of Judah.

# CHAPTER EIGHT: JEWISH GOVERNMENT IN THE TIME OF JESUS

To understand the rise of Christianity, and also the rise of our form of Rabbinic Judaism, it is helpful to understand government in the Land of Israel in the First Century. This is a complicated topic as there were many levels of government and competing sources of authority.

Judea was a province of the Roman Empire. The Romans ruled the entire Mediterranean world. As with all ancient empires, the subject peoples of Rome were entitled to their own national rulers. They lived under their own laws and by their customary practices and religions. The subject peoples were expected to keep the peace, pay their taxes and obey the Emperor. The Romans engaged in direct rule when they found it necessary, as was the case with some regions of Judea in the time of Jesus.

## Hasmonean Kings and High Priests

For centuries, under the Persian and then Greek Empires, the Jews of the province of Judah had lived their traditional life under the rule of the High Priest. The High Priest presided over the rites of the Jerusalem Temple and was also the temporal ruler of the Jews. The High Priest was a lineal descendant of Zadok, who was High Priest in the time of King David.

This traditional way of life came to an end with the events that are well known from the celebration of Hannukah. Judah Maccabee led a revolt against the Greek king Antiochus, who had outlawed the Torah. Judah was a member of the Hasmonean priestly family. They were hereditary priests, but not in the line of Zadok. In the decades after the successful rebellion, Judah's brother Simon established himself as King and High Priest in Jerusalem. Simon was not of the High Priestly line and certainly not of Davidic royal descent. Furthermore, the Torah establishes the Kingship and the High

Priesthood as separate entities; they had never been combined in one person. Many Jews objected to the Hasmonean rulers. On the positive side, the Hasmoneans did establish independence for Judah as the Greek Empire crumbled, and they extended the boundaries of the kingdom to the tribal boundaries of ancient Israel.

**Herod the Great**

Eighty years of independence came to an end when a Hasmonean claimant to the throne invited the Roman general Pompey into Jerusalem to fight for his cause. The Romans were only too happy to come, and then they stayed. After some years the Romans removed the contentious Hasmoneans from rulership and placed on the throne of Judea a favorite of their own, Herod, remembered in history as Herod the Great. Herod married Mariamne, "the last of the Hasmoneans", to provide himself with a veneer of legitimacy. He later had her killed and he took other wives.

Herod skillfully managed the various factions of his subjects, Jewish and Gentile, while he remained a favorite in Rome. He was one of the great architects and builders of all time. He built the port city of Caesarea as the Roman capital of Judea, with a magnificent palace for himself. He built the fortress of Masada, a tourist site today, on a mesa above the Dead Sea, as a redoubt for himself in case of local rebellion or an invasion by Cleopatra of Egypt, who desired to rule over Judea herself. Herod's grandest project was the reconstruction of the Jerusalem Temple. Herod made the Temple one of the grandest buildings in the Roman Empire. The workers were still putting the finishing touches on the building when the Great Rebellion broke out in 66 CE. The Romans burned the Second Temple in July of the year 70 (the 9th of Av), bringing the biblically ordained sacrifices to an end forever.

Herod was brutal to his family, killing a wife and three sons, but he was an able ruler. Herod did keep kosher, and jokesters in Rome said of Herod that "it was better to be his pig than his son." His subjects enjoyed some decades of peace and prosperity. He did not ever order the death of all the babies born at the time of Jesus; this is a legend designed to associate baby Jesus with the Torah story of baby Moses and Pharaoh.

## Roman Rule

After the death of Herod, the Romans could not find anyone capable to rule his kingdom. The Romans divided Herod's kingdom into four parts. One of his sons, Herod Antipater, was granted rule over the Galilee, though without the title of king. That made Jesus a subject of Antipater. The Romans ruled over the region of Judea directly, through prefects. These were Roman bureaucrats assigned to administrate the region. During brief periods the Romans appointed Jewish kings over Judah, such as Agrippa from 41-44, but mostly the Romans ruled through the prefects, who were Romans not Jews. Although Pontius Pilate is called a procurator in the New Testament, he was actually a prefect, which is a lower level official. Josephus tells us that the prefects were almost all incompetent and brutal, especially two named Felix and Pontius Pilate. This is the Pontius Pilate who condemned Jesus to death.

In the meantime, the High Priesthood continued. The High Priests were nominally the highest authority over the Jews of Judea. The Romans auctioned off the High Priesthood on a regular basis to candidates from amongst the high-born priestly families. The High Priest had to wear his priestly vestments in order to officiate over the rites of the Temple. The Romans kept the vestments in the Antonia Fortress, which was next to the Temple courtyard. The High Priest had to go each morning to collect the vestments and return them each night. In this way the Romans made it clear who was really in charge. Jews still

not survive the destruction of the Temple, they had no one to positively represent their point of view for the judgment of history.

The Pharisees opposed the power of the Hasmonean kings, who executed many of them. On one occasion King Alexander Yannai lined the road from the seacoast to Jerusalem with crucified Pharisees. Crucifixion was a Greek form of execution, which the Hasmonean rulers adopted for their political opponents. Rabbinic legend tells us that on his deathbed Yannai instructed his wife, Queen Regent Salome, to support the Pharisees due to their popularity with the public. From that time on the Pharisees stayed out of conflict with the power groups and focused on their own agenda. Salome is remembered in the Talmud as Queen Sh'lom-Tsion. She has a street named after her in modern Jerusalem to honor her role in saving the Pharisees.

The Essenes were a breakaway from the Sadducee movement. They represent out-of-power priests who were disgusted with the Hasmonean Temple leadership. The Essenes created a desert retreat where they lived out a fantasy life of how the Jewish people would live if they had a proper high priest. They contrasted their leader, the Teacher of Righteousness, with the standing high priest whom they titled the Wicked Priest. We do not know if the Teacher of Righteousness was the founder of the Essenes or the title for every leader in turn. The Essenes were organized in religious and military hierarchy, ready for a cosmic battle at the coming end time when their project would be fulfilled. The Essenes had strict rules about Jewish observance and ritual purity. They would not engage in sexual relations nor would they defecate within the city walls of Jerusalem, the Holy City. They would not defecate at all on the Sabbath. Josephus amusingly records that the Essenes of Jerusalem could be seen waddling hurriedly on the way to their latrines outside the city gates on Saturday night. The Essenes seem to be the authors of the Dead Sea Scrolls, which contain their sectarian writings as well as books of the Bible. The Essenes apparently joined the Great Rebellion against the Romans and were wiped out.

## Sanhedrin

In the Chamber of Hewn Stones within the walls of the Temple met a Jewish council, called the Sanhedrin. As indicated by its Greek name, the Sanhedrin goes back to Greek times. According to rabbinic tradition, the Sanhedrin had 71 members. The president was called the Nasi, "exalted one" and the vice president was called the Av Bet Din, "father of the court." They faced the other 69 members who sat in a semi-circle. According to rabbinic tradition recorded in the Talmud, the early Sages ran the Temple and Jewish life in general through their control of the Sanhedrin.

Contemporary historians doubt the Talmudic account. As long as the Temple stood, the High Priest was most likely in control, even if the Pharisees were not pleased with his leadership. Contemporary historians believe that the Sanhedrin of the Temple was most likely a privy council to the High Priest. Its members were chosen not because of their wisdom in Torah learning, as the Talmud would have it, but because they came from noble, priestly or powerful families. In the ancient world, status derived from birth.

After the destruction of the Temple, Rabban Yohanan ben Zakkai and his circle of Sages reconstituted the Sanhedrin in the village of Yavneh on the coastal plain below Jerusalem. The members of this Sanhedrin were called Rabbi, the first formal use of that title. The Nasi was addressed as Rabban, "our rabbi." In this Sanhedrin the Pharisees apparently predominated, though the title Pharisee soon lost meaning as the Rabbis centralized their leadership. This Sanhedrin in Yavneh was the council of Sages which the Talmud projects backward into the Temple days. Once the sects disappeared, the opposing parties in the Sanhedrin were the School of Hillel and the School of Shammai. Hillel and Shammai were Sages who lived in the generation prior to Jesus.

After the year 70 there was no longer a king or prefect over Judea. The Romans ruled Judea directly as a sub-province of Syria. There was no longer a High Priest. The factions of Sadducee, Pharisee and Essene and any others ceased to exist. The Rabbis exerted their authority over all Jews, backed by the Romans, while Christianity became a Gentile religion and moved away from any relationship with Jewish authority.

The rabbinic Sanhedrin of Yavneh lasted until the Bar Kochba rebellion against the Roman Empire in 132-35. After the Bar Kochba rebellion the Sanhedrin reconstituted itself in the Galilee, where it lasted until the Fourth Century, when it was finally suppressed by the Christian Emperors of Rome. Jewish authority then passed to the rabbinical academies of Babylon, under the neo-Persian Empire, out of the reach of the Christian authorities.

Who sat in the Sanhedrin, and by what right did they sit there? Premodern Jews assumed as the Talmud states that the Sanhedrin was always a council of Sages. According to Fourth Century Jewish sources, Hillel was Nasi and Shammai was Av Ben Din around the time of Herod's rule. Hillel and Shammai are remembered in Talmudic tradition as *Avot Haolam*, "the Founding Fathers" of Judaism as we know it. They were credited with establishing rabbinic rule against the will of the High Priests.

The modern study of ancient Judaism began in the Nineteenth Century. This was an era when democracy was spreading in Europe through the establishment of national parliaments, often under the rule of a monarch or prince. The English model of this form of government exists to the present day. The Queen is nominal ruler while Parliament runs the country.

Nineteenth Century Jews were excited by parliamentary rule, which promised greater rights for Jews than they had enjoyed under Medieval style feudal governments. Jewish historians of the time thought of the Sanhedrin as a parliament for ancient Judea. The Jews were two thousand years ahead of their time, establishing a parliamentary democracy to rule the country under the nominal leadership of the High Priest, the King and the Romans. Jewish and Christian historians of the late 19<sup>th</sup> and early 20<sup>th</sup> Centuries wrote of the sects of Judaism, the Sadducees and Pharisees and Essenes, as if they were political parties. It was presumed that every Jew was a member of one party or another, like European people of modern times. Hillel must have been head of the majority Pharisee party, with the Sadducee, Shammai, leading the loyal opposition. There was speculation about which party Jesus might have belonged to, whether he voted with the Pharisees as a disciple of Hillel, or perhaps with the Essenes.

We may be amused by the political enthusiasm of the historians of that era, but there is no support for their suppositions. Contemporary historians understand that the sects were leadership groups. Most Jews of the time were just Jews, not involved in political intrigue or fine points of religious doctrine. Jesus comes into contact with Pharisees and Sadducees only when he enters Jerusalem, not in the environs of Nazareth. Hillel and Shammai are never identified with any party or institution. They are not called "rabbi", as the title did not exist in their time. They are remembered only by the non-specific honorific "Elder." They may not have sat in the Sanhedrin at all. It is possible that in their time they were leaders of schools of thought, probably Pharisaic thought. Only after the year 70, when the disciples of their schools took practices. The second possible reconstruction adopts the "historian's assumption" that the Mishnah represents a late Second Century rabbinic fantasy of Temple jurisprudence. The Mishnah shows how the rabbis would have run the Temple had they been in charge. Historians say that we must reconstruct Jesus' trial from all available evidence of First Century Judaism, much of which contradicts the Mishnah.

## Jesus' Trial as Recorded in the Synoptic Gospels

Before we proceed, let us review the outline of Jesus' arrest and trial, as presented consistently in the three Synoptic Gospels. Jesus was arrested on the first night of Passover. The arresting officers were of the Temple guard, or possibly Roman troops. Jesus was brought before the Sanhedrin, a Jewish high court, where he was tried that very night. The Gospels say that the High Priest, Joseph Caiphas, presided over the trial. The Jewish court was anxious to convict Jesus, possibly because they feared he would stir up the crowd and cause a riot which would lead to the Romans' killing of many Jews. They are also accused of envy. The court found Jesus guilty of blasphemy and condemned him to death. Since they had no power to carry out the sentence they turned Jesus over to Pontius Pilate, the Roman governor of Judea. Pilate may have sent Jesus to his king, Herod Antipater (the ruler of Galilee, who was in Jerusalem for the Passover holiday), for a hearing. If so, Herod returned him to Pilate. Pilate found the man innocent, but condemned him to death upon the insistence of the Jewish leaders. According to the Gospel of Matthew the entire Jewish people stood outside the court, crying "Crucify him, and his blood be upon us and our descendants." (Matt. 27:23-25) Pontius Pilate washed his hands to demonstrate his innocence and then ordered the crucifixion of Jesus. Jesus was scourged, then crucified. The sign over his head announcing his "crime" stated "King of the Jews".

78

## Analysis of the Trial Using Mishnaic Law

From what the Mishnah tells us about Jewish law there are some problems with the trial story as it stands.

The Gospels say that the Sanhedrin found Jesus guilty of blasphemy. Yet none of Jesus' words or deeds are blasphemous according to Jewish law. It was not blasphemy to claim to be the Messiah or to claim that one could knock down and rebuild the Temple by God's hand. If anything, these were claims of Jewish piety! The only crime of "blasphemy" according to the Mishnah is misuse of the holy divine name, YHWH (Mishnah Sanhedrin 7:5). Jesus was never accused of this, so he could not have been found guilty of blasphemy.

Jesus could not have been tried on a capital offense in the manner told in the Gospel. According to the Mishnah there were many judicial rules designed to protect defendants accused of a capital crime (Sanhedrin 4:1). The trial had to be held before a full court. Conviction required a majority of at least two, but if all the judges voted to convict the defendant was acquitted. Both the trial and the sentencing hearing had to be held during the daylight hours. The court could not convict on the day of the trial. They had to hear evidence one day and vote on the next day.

Jewish courts did not meet on festival or Sabbath days according to the Mishnah. Since a capital case required a two-day trial, no capital trial was initiated on the eve of a festival. This contradicts both the Synoptics' timetable and John's.

We must conclude from this evidence that Jesus was not tried by a legally established Jewish court. He must have been tried by a kangaroo court called together by the High Priest Caiphas, a notorious lackey of the Romans. Caiphas must have been acting on orders from the Romans, who wanted Jesus dead because they feared he would foment a rebellion.

it must have been because Pontius Pilate wanted to exercise Roman authority in this case.

We know from Josephus that Pontius Pilate slaughtered numerous innocent Jews. It is unlikely in the extreme that he would have had any scruples about executing Jesus, whether he thought Jesus innocent or guilty. He most likely gave no thought to crucifying one who was, in his eyes, just another Jewish rebel, a man who had become dangerous.

The conclusion of the historians: Jesus was killed by some Romans and some Jews, a conspiracy between the homegrown and imperial rulers of the country, in order to keep the peace during the Passover holiday.

**Why Was Jesus Killed?**

What was the charge against Jesus? We surmise that Caiphas and Pilate believed that Jesus either intended an insurrection, or else he would be the cause of one. Proclaiming the Kingdom of God was anti-Roman, whether the proclaimer expected the Kingdom to come by armed rebellion or by divine intervention. After all John the Baptist was universally admired, yet he was killed just because he was attracting crowds. Apocalyptic teachings in one sense encourage political passivity; the Elect must serve God faithfully and await the unfolding of the divine plan. Yet in another sense apocalyptic teaching is radical and explosive, since it raises hopes and expectations for social change to a fever pitch. The Romans were aware of this. Jesus threatened their peace. Around the time of Jesus, the Romans cut down a person named Theudas and his four hundred followers, though they had done nothing more noxious than go out into the desert to await divine deliverance.

We can see from the above that no specific word or deed of Jesus was needed for the High Priest and the Romans to feel threatened by him. Yet, there may have been a specific cause. It is conjecture, but not unlikely, that the arrest and trial of

Jesus was related to Jesus' action in driving the money-changers and pigeon sellers out of the Temple.

This act of Jesus is hard for moderns to comprehend. The money-changers were providing a necessary service. People came to the Temple from all over. They needed local currency to pay their Temple dues, as required by Jewish piety. Jesus' action can be better understood in terms of the Hellenistic attitude to those who made money with money. The philosopher Aristotle had asked "What is money?" His answer: "Money is nothing." Those who make money with money were making something from nothing. This, said Aristotle, is unethical. We moderns think of money as a commodity to be invested for profit. Ancients thought differently.

The money-changers, though necessary, may have seemed an affront to economic justice, right there in the porticos of God's holy Temple.

There is something missing from the "cleansing of the Temple" story in the Gospels. The money-changers and pigeon-sellers had a legal right to have their stalls in the Temple. They had probably even paid rent for the space. The Temple had a large guard to protect public order and the huge Temple treasury. At festival seasons like the Passover the Temple was also surrounded by Roman soldiers who were constantly on the lookout for trouble. The Jews had learned to tolerate the Roman military presence as long as the soldiers were respectful. Jesus could not have driven out the money-changers with whips unless he were protected by a group of followers that was large enough and sufficiently well-armed to protect him from arrest.

Some scholars are aware of this historical difficulty in the text but are reluctant, for reasons of their own, to attribute any militancy to Jesus. They have suggested that Jesus held the worse, who would willingly bring a curse and condemnation down upon the heads of their own innocent children?

We may not be able to reconstruct the causes of Matthew's accusation against the Jews, but let us remember that Matthew is the Gospel writer who most desires to keep Christianity within the fold of the Jewish religion. He is a loyal Jew and he depicts Jesus as a loyal Jew. Matthew could not possibly have intended the suffering that his attributed saying has caused to his own people. Matthew's passion story may have originated as sacred theater. The Christian audience cries for Jesus' blood to be upon their heads. The audience experiences sin, condemnation and the grace of God's forgiveness as they recreate the Passion of Christ.

**The Passion Story and the Bible**

Much of the Passion story is a *midrash*, an interpretation of Scripture. The events may be factual in outline, but the way they are retold is intended to call to mind certain Scriptural passages which, according to the Evangelists, were fulfilled in Jesus' Passion. The Passion story was composed with two Bible passages especially in mind - Isaiah 53 (the "suffering servant" passage) and Psalm 22. Jesus was crucified beside other political prisoners. The Gospel identifies them as "criminals" to fulfill the verse in Isaiah 53:12 "he was numbered among the sinners". The story of the Roman soldiers who cast lots for Jesus' cloak is based on Psalm 22:19.

Many have been mystified by the report of Jesus' final words on the cross: "My God, my God, why have you forsaken me?" (Psalm 22:1). Luke and John report different words. Possibly they are scandalized by Jesus' seeming expression of despair. But it is possible that Jesus was not expressing despair at all. He was quoting the first verse of Psalm 22. (Whether he truly did so or whether the Gospel places the words in his mouth is not material to the message.) A Jew in Jesus' time would know this Psalm. The first line is sufficient to call to memory the entire Psalm, which begins with despair and concludes in triumphant self-assurance and divine praise. The point of the quote is that Jesus, dying on the cross, is confident that God has saved him. His death is a victory.

## A Heart-Rending Fantasy

Elie Wiesel, the Nobel Peace Prize winning writer and Auschwitz survivor, imagines the following conversation in Jerusalem between an unbalanced Holocaust survivor and Jesus:

It is now Shlomo's turn to speak: "May I tell you about my meeting with Yeoshua? Do you remember him? The innocent preacher who had only one word on his lips: love. Poor man. I saw him the day he was crucified. Not far from here." ....

I remember it clearly. I went over to him and said: 'It is not you I shall be waiting for.' He seemed serene, at peace with himself and the whole creation. I tried to make him understand that this was not the first time a Jew was dying for his faith. There were other martyrs before him. But they had gone to their death crying, screaming with pain. For them, for us, no death is worthy of being invoked or sanctified. All life is sacred, irreplaceable; it is inhuman for any person to renounce it joyfully, it is blasphemous to abandon it without remorse.

"'Are you angry with me?' he asked.

"'No,' I answered. Not angry. Just sad.'

"'Because of me?'

"'Yes, because of you. You think you are suffering for my sake and for my brothers', yet we are the ones who will be made to suffer for you, because of you.'

"Since he refused to believe this, I began to describe what actions his followers would undertake in his name to spread his

87

word. I painted a picture of the future which made him see the innumerable victims persecuted and crushed under the sign of his law. Thereupon he burst into tears of despair: 'No, no! This is not how it will be! You are wrong, you must be! This is not how I foresee the reign of my spirit! I want my heritage to be a gift of compassion and hope, not a punishment in blood!' His sobs broke my heart and I sought to comfort him. (*A Beggar in Jerusalem*, Random House, NY, 1970, pp.56-57)

## Recent History

In 1963 the Catholic Church published a document called *Nostra Aetate* which was a new teaching about the Jews. The publication of this document was part of the larger Second Vatican Council which was intended to update the Church on many fronts. In the *Nostra Aetate* document the Church stated that the Jews of today are not to be blamed for the death of Jesus. Christians should remember that Jesus died willingly in order to fulfill his mission. This pronouncement was met with great joy by Jews. In America, the Church reacted swiftly to remove from all of its textbooks and teachings any mention of blame upon the Jews for the death of Jesus. The Church in other countries was slower to react, but gradually this accusation has died out. Most younger Catholics, at least in America, would be surprised to learn that the Jews had ever been blamed. The text in the Gospel of Matthew remains, but as with all biblical writings it is all a matter of how the Bible is taught and which portions are emphasized and which intentionally overlooked. Jews quote Isaiah all the time, "Let them beat their swords into plowshares", but never quote Joel when he reverses Isaiah and says "Let them beat their plowshares into swords." In like manner it has been possible for the Church to change its teaching on the Jews, regardless of certain biblical passages.

Since *Nostra Aetate* various Protestant churches in America have published similar statements. Let us hope that the accusation of deicide against the Jews belongs firmly in the historical past. In the years since the Holocaust steps have been taken so dramatic and transformative that Christian-Jewish relations can never go back.

single God who created and rules over the universe, dispensing justice to human beings. Monotheists all believe, each in their own way, that God's ultimate plan is the salvation of humankind.

## Polytheism vs Monotheism

Monotheism differs from polytheism in more than the number of deities. The One of the One God is not just the lowest possible number in a series like one, two, three. If God is one, that means that Unity is the highest principle in the universe. All dualities and irreconcilable paradoxes are merely appearances. Above them all stands a higher unity, even if it is not apparent in daily life. The One God assures that Justice prevails in the end. In polytheistic religion the gods also demonstrate an interest in justice, but they are motivated by their own interests which often brings them into conflict with other gods. Conflict rather than unity is part of ultimate reality. The gods can be fickle. Odysseus, for example, runs into many impediments on his way home from the Trojan War, a journey that takes ten years, because he has angered the god Poseidon. He may never have made it home but for the favor of the goddess Athena. The conflict of these two gods determines what happens to Odysseus more than his own righteousness or lack thereof. Above the personal conflict of all the gods stand the Fates, who inscrutably determine the successes and failures of each human being. Oedipus was fated to murder his father and marry his mother, and neither gods nor human effort could change that fate. In monotheism, God makes the ultimate decision. It could be argued that polytheism explains better than monotheism the vagaries of human existence. That is why monotheism requires a leap of faith to perceive an ultimate unity and justice in the world. The search by scientists for a Unified Field Theory that explains in one equation the four fundamental forces in the universe expresses in a secular way a monotheistic belief in an overarching cosmic Unity. Such a theory has proven elusive but scientists believe in it as a matter of faith.

## Gnosticism – Two Powers

Monotheism and polytheism are not the only possible choices. A third type of religion, Gnosticism, powerfully influenced the evolution of the three monotheistic faiths. Gnosticism is a term used to describe the belief in two gods, a god of good and a god of evil. The religion of the ancient Persian Empire was dualistic. This Gnostic faith is called Zoroastrianism after its founding prophet, Zoroaster. There are still some Zoroastrians in the world today, though the spread of Islam suppressed the religion almost totally. The ongoing influence of Gnosticism has been not through formally Gnostic religions, most of which have died out, but through the influence of Gnostic ideas within Judaism, Christianity and Islam.

In Gnostic religion the contrary forces of good and evil are in constant conflict over the world. In Gnostic religion the evil god, not the good god, created the world. The good god rules over the immaterial world of the spirit. As human beings become immersed in material and earthly pursuits, they attach themselves to the force of evil. As human beings rise above the material world and become spiritual, they attach themselves to the good god. Gnosis means knowledge. In Gnostic religion there is a secret knowledge known to the true worshipers. Possession of this knowledge enables one to rise above materialism and live within the good world of spirit.

The term Gnostic is sometimes used to describe specific religious movements. Here we use the term in a generic sense to describe any religion that is based upon a dualistic conflict between the ultimate powers of good and evil and upon a radical distinction between material and spiritual being, with rites and beliefs that enable access to the spiritual realm.

93

## The Rabbis Battle Gnosticism

The earliest Rabbis shaped our form of Judaism after the destruction of the Second Temple in the year 70. The Rabbis worked hard to suppress all forms of sectarian Judaism which disagreed with their perspective. The early Jewish Christians met their disapproval, but the Christian group for a long time was very small and relatively powerless. The main opponent of Rabbinic Judaism was Gnostic Judaism. The Rabbis were devoted monotheists. They worked hard to suppress Gnostic beliefs amongst their fellow Jews. When Rabbinic writings denounce *minim* – sectarians – historians think that these texts in most cases are directed against Gnostics, not Christians.

A primary belief of Gnostics is that the material world is created and ruled by the evil deity, the *demiurge,* while the good deity rules over the spirit. In their opposition to Gnosticism, the Rabbis opposed anti-material beliefs. The Rabbis taught rather that a Jew should use both material and spiritual gifts in the service of God. The Rabbis opposed celibacy and total abstinence from alcohol because they saw this as calling "evil" that which God has called "good." It is notable that Judaism is almost unique among world religions in having no form of monasticism. Opposition to Gnostic beliefs got another push in Judaism in the Middle Ages. Maimonides, whose philosophy totally transformed the religion, was an adamant monotheist.

To keep Jews of today further confused, belief in the Devil and in Hell persisted in Judaism. One finds references to it in Jewish writings from all ages. But this belief persisted primarily in the folk tradition and did not become a mainstream or required belief in Judaism. Maimonides teaches that the souls of evil people, when they die, dissolve and do not participate in that reward which is reserved for the righteous. There is no Hell fire for them.

## Gnosticism and Kabbalah

There is a Hell in the Zohar (published around 1280), the central text of Jewish mysticism, the Kabbalah. While there is no Devil in the Zohar, the Snake in the Garden of Eden plays that role, obviously influenced by Christian teaching. In Kabbalah there is a demonic world as a mirror image to the world of goodness, ruled over by a king and queen of the demons, Samael and Lilith. The great Twentieth Century scholar of Kabbalah, Gershom Scholem, said that Kabbalah represents a full-blown reappearance of Gnosticism in Judaism, centuries after the Rabbis had suppressed it. Scholem speculated on the unanswerable question of whether Gnosticism was reinvented in Medieval Kabbalah or whether a secret strand of Gnosticism continued to exist in Judaism from ancient times without generating any written evidence until the Thirteenth Century.

Martin Buber, perhaps the other greatest Jewish scholar of the Twentieth Century, claimed that the Eighteenth Century movement of Hasidism purged Gnostic beliefs from Kabbalah. Scholem strongly disagreed with Buber. It is true that the Baal Shem Tov, the founder of Hasidism, taught that a Hasid should enjoy eating and drinking and rejoicing in this world, but the ideological teachings of Hasidism are as Gnostic as those of earlier Kabbalah. Spirituality is consistently contrasted to material concerns in Hasidic teaching. The fact of poverty in the lives of most Hasidim was elevated into a virtue which leads one to holiness. Many Hasidim wore a *gartle* around their waist, a belt whose function was to separate the holy upper body from the unholy lower body. Scholem's view is probably the correct view.

One sees that in every age the prejudice in official Judaism was against Gnosticism, but at the same time Jews were often attracted by the power of Gnostic beliefs.

# CHAPTER ELEVEN: THE MONOTHEISTIC FAITHS

Jews in the modern world are proud of being the original monotheistic religion, the source and inspiration for Christianity and Islam. Many Jews were raised to see Judaism as the mother religion, with Christianity and Islam as her two daughters. Some recent Christian historians of religion have argued that it would be more accurate to see Judaism, Christianity and Islam as three sister religions. Let us explore the facts behind both claims.

One can see why Jews would lay claim to having the mother religion. Chronologically, Judaism came first. By the time Christianity came along the Jews had a history that they traced back to Father Abraham, about 1700 BCE in the Middle Bronze Age. The era of the giving of the Torah at Mt. Sinai is placed at about 1200 BCE.

Judaism was evolving throughout the Second Temple Era, which spanned from 500 BCE to 70 CE. Jesus was born into a Jewish nation in a Jewish land that already looked back on a history of many centuries. Jesus was a Jew and all of his earliest followers were Jews. Jesus and his followers spoke Aramaic and understood Hebrew. Their holy Scriptures were the Torah and Prophets of the Hebrew Bible. Their frame of reference for the world was Jewish. Only some years after the crucifixion of Jesus did the religion founded in his name become a Greek speaking religion of Gentiles.

Even after Christianity became the religion of the Roman Empire, Judaism was still the original reference point for Christians in a multitude of ways. Christians adopted the Hebrew Bible as part of their Holy Scriptures. The Christian Bible, the New Testament, makes so many references to Jews, Judaism and the Hebrew Bible that it would not be comprehensible without Judaism. Paul, as he explains the meaning of the Christ and Christianity in his Epistles, does so by comparison and contrast with Judaism.

The Christian holidays of Easter and Pentecost are based upon the Jewish holidays of Passover and Shavuot. In most languages, Easter is called Passover. The symbolism of these holidays is built upon the symbolism of the Jewish holidays. We do not know why Christians do not observe the third Jewish festival of Sukkot, but the palm branches of Sukkot were carried over into the Easter celebration. The Christian order of worship is based on the Jewish order of worship as it developed in the last years of the Second Temple.

When Jews think about our influence upon the Christian world, we recall the Jewishness of Jesus and the Christian adoption of the Jewish Bible. The Ten Commandments in our Torah are the basis for morality in the Christian world as well, along with the commandment to love your neighbor as yourself. There is another influence so pervasive that we take it for granted – the adoption by Christians and Muslims of the Jewish week. One reads many theories about the innovation of the week, but the only function of the week is to measure the days from one Sabbath to the next. The Jews gave to the world a day of rest once every seven days. We take the week for granted, but there is no suggestion of it in nature, and in those societies which do not measure time by the week people work constantly, except on occasional holidays.

Paul told Christians to observe the Ten Commandments, which includes the Sabbath day. Gradually Christians differentiated themselves by observing instead the first day of the week as the Lord's Day. Sunday is not historically a day of absolute rest like the Jewish Sabbath, but it is a day for worship and relaxation. When Islam came along some centuries later the Muslims also adopted the week and took Friday as the Muslim day of worship.

Islam also adopted many of its beliefs and customs from Judaism, as well as from Christianity. One may debate whether certain Muslim customs were learned by Mohammed by his observation of Jews or of Christians. The very idea of a single transcendent God is a prime influence, which Islam takes even farther than Judaism and Christianity. Muslims worship five times a day, which almost certainly derives from Judaism. Jews recite five prayer liturgies a day – two Shema and three Tefilah – although for a long time these have been merged into three or two prayer sessions. The Koran retells many Bible stories and Talmudic sayings, although in its own way. The Muslim claim is that the Koran is giving the corrected version of these teachings and stories, which is a backwards acknowledgment of indebtedness to Judaism. To a historian much in Islam seems based upon Jewish and Christian models, but to a faithful Muslim all of Islam is based upon divine revelations to Mohammed, the founding prophet of Islam. Islam does acknowledge Abraham, Moses, and other Jewish biblical heroes, as well as Jesus, as early prophets of God who exist in the chain of prophecy that culminates in Mohammed.

We have observed how Judaism can be seen as the mother of the three monotheistic religions. What is the evidence for the "three sisters" perspective? Even if Judaism is chronologically first, can we say that the influence has been all in one direction? Jews have lived surrounded by Christians, and then by Christians and Muslims, for 1,700 years. Judaism has grown and evolved continually during those years, which constitute more than half of all time going back to Abraham and Sarah. Has not the evolution of Judaism been strongly influenced by the majority populations amongst whom we have lived?

Judaism at the time of Jesus came in different forms. The various sects of Judaism had differing beliefs and practices. The Greek speaking Jews of the Diaspora in the Roman Empire had their own version of Judaism which often differed in important details from the practices of the Aramaic speaking Jews of the Land of Israel and Babylon. Christianity did not break away from a single unified Judaism. It is likely that Christianity in its origins picked up some strains of sectarian Judaism that were abandoned or rejected by the Rabbinic brand of Judaism. Late Second Temple Judaism can be looked at as a bouillabaisse, a broth with lots of meaty chunks in it. Rabbinical Judaism picked out some chunks, while the early Christian Church selected other chunks. Seen this way, Christianity and Rabbinical Judaism are equal descendants of earlier Judaism. Jews would claim more continuity for Judaism than for Christianity. The Jews maintained the ethnic and national identity of the Jewish people, while Christianity became the international religion of many people whose relationship to the biblical Israelites is one of spiritual connection alone. Jews and Christians have debated, not always in a friendly manner, over which religion can lay claim to the non-Scriptural writings of the Second Temple Era – the Dead Sea Scrolls, the Apocrypha and Pseudepigrapha. Some Christians claimed that these documents represent a continuity from the Hebrew Bible to the New Testament which bypassed Judaism. The most common Jewish retort is that these documents are too sectarian to be central to the historical thread. There is more than one way of interpreting the historical evidence. There is reason to say that Christianity could be seen as a sister religion to Judaism.

Aside from the positive influences, the anti-Jewish assertions of Christianity have also influenced Judaism in ways that are impossible to evaluate, since we can never know what Judaism would have become if not for the honing that came from a constant defensive posture. What would have been the eventual disposition of Jewish messianic beliefs, of beliefs about divine forgiveness and the value of mitzvot, if not for the need to respond to Christian arguments against Judaism? In the

Fourteenth Century the Spanish Jewish scholar Nachmanides, finding himself unable to defend Judaism against claims based on the Aggadah, the non-legal teachings of Judaism, responded by denigrating Aggadah relative to the legal aspects of Judaism, the Halacha. If not for the Medieval disputations, perhaps Judaism would have evolved from that point based more on Aggadah and less on Halacha. We will never know.

Judaism has been influenced more by Christianity and Islam than many traditional Jews would like to admit. The Zohar, central text of the Kabbalah, demonstrates a great debt to Medieval Spanish Catholicism. As one simple example, the Kabbalistic custom of midnight study and prayer is derived from the monastic custom of midnight chanting. The Zohar even acknowledges that such a custom exists "amongst the nations." The great Jewish philosophers of the Middle Ages learned philosophy from the Muslims. Saadia Gaon based his Jewish philosophy on the Islamic Mutakalimun. Maimonides learned how to apply the philosophy of Aristotle to monotheistic religion from Averroes. Thomas Aquinas drew from both Maimonides and Averroes.

If Judaism is the mother, she is a mother who has learned a lot from her daughters. I prefer the image of mother and daughters, having learned this as a child as a source of Jewish pride. Even so it must be acknowledged that there is a lot of evidence to support the view that Judaism, Christianity and Islam are three sister religions. They have evolved in relation to one another. None of the three religions is possible to imagine in its present form without the existence of the others.

# CHAPTER TWELVE: THE JERUSALEM TEMPLE

## Jewish Religion in the Time of the Temple

In one sense, Judaism and Christianity are two opposing answers to the question, "What replaces animal sacrifice after the destruction of the Temple?". We cannot fully understand Judaism or Christianity, or their relationship, without knowing about the Temple and what it meant to Jews while it stood and after it was gone.

Many Christians think of Judaism as "the religion of the Old Testament" but every Jew knows how misleading that is. The religion described in the Old Testament is a religion in which hereditary priests offer up animal sacrifices to God on behalf of Israelite farmers. The hereditary priests of Old Testament times are now your neighbors the Cohens, who make a living just like everybody else. The animal sacrifices, along with the altar, the incense and the menorah lamp, are a distant memory. The religious practices described in the Torah for the most part no longer exist. Judaism has evolved and changed since Old Testament times. The greatest turning point in that evolution is the destruction of the Jerusalem Temple by the Romans in summer of the year 70 CE.

The earliest Israelites offered sacrifices to God in various locations around the Land of Israel. In the time of the Assyrian threat King Hezekiah centralized the worship in Jerusalem and prohibited sacrifice in any other place. From the time of Hezekiah, the Jews understood that they could sacrifice only in Jerusalem, nowhere else.

Sacrifices ceased for seventy years during the Babylonian Exile, after King Nebukadnezzer destroyed Solomon's Temple on the 9th day of the month of Av in the year 586 BCE. It seems that the Jews of Babylon were careful to observe the

105

Sabbath, keep kosher, and marry amongst themselves. This was their survival strategy and their religion. As soon as the Persians permitted the Jews to reestablish Judah and Jerusalem within the Persian Empire, the Jews rebuilt the Temple and restored the service of animal sacrifice.

There were Jews who had seen the First Temple as children who saw the Second Temple in their old age. The Second Temple structure was rebuilt a number of times. The ultimate Second Temple was that built by King Herod. He enlarged the entire mountain top to make a bigger space for his grand Temple project. The Western Wall at which Jews pray today is the remains of Herod's retaining wall around the Temple Mount. This grand Temple was barely finished when the Jews rebelled against Rome in 66 CE. The Roman general Titus, when he concluded the conquest of Jerusalem in 70CE, burned down the Temple on the 9th of Av, the same date as the destruction of the First Temple. The Temple was never rebuilt. Jewish sacrifice came to a sudden end.

The Second Temple went through a period of crisis in 168 BCE when King Antiochus IV, the Greek king of the Middle East, outlawed the Torah and placed a statue of a Greek god, probably Zeus, in the Temple. He had pigs sacrificed to this idol on the Temple altar. The Maccabee rebels reclaimed the Temple three years later. They purified the Temple and reestablished the worship of God.

We have already seen how many Jews had little esteem for the high priests during the last decades of the Second Temple. Some of these Jews, like the Pharisees and the Essenes, developed alternatives to the priesthood and the Temple service. The Essenes had a substitute priesthood ready to take over the Temple after the final war between the forces of good and evil. Events turned out differently. Without a Temple, the

Essenes disappeared, along with the Sadducees and any other Jewish sect which was centered on the Temple sacrifices.

## Surviving the Destruction of the Temple – What Replaces Sacrifice?

The Pharisees and the Christians survived the destruction of the year 70 because they had alternative programs for the service of God that were not dependent upon the sacrifices.

The destruction of the Temple was the most notable event of the First Century for Christians as well as Jews. It might be hard for Christians of our time to realize it, but the death of Jesus on the cross was not much noted in its time. The Resurrection was an article of faith in the early Christian community but did not create a sensation outside of that circle. The Gospels acknowledge as much; the miracle of Christianity is partly that it grew from obscurity to such renown. In the year 70 the earliest Christians, notably Paul, were still working out the meaning of Jesus' death on the cross and developing the doctrine of the Christ. After the destruction of the Temple the question for Christians became, "What is the meaning of the Christ in light of the end of animal sacrifice?"

## The Christian Answer

The destruction of the Temple captured the world's attention. Christianity grew in part because it had a satisfactory response to the destruction. The answer of Christianity is that the death of Jesus on the cross was the perfect sacrifice that provides atonement for human sins. Faith in the Christ is participation in the perfect sacrificial offering. Once God had sacrificed God's own self as a human offering, there was no more need for animal sacrifices. God swept away the Temple when it had been replaced by the sacrifice of Jesus. This answer, as history shows, did not capture the imagination of Jews, but it did capture the imagination of Gentiles. As Gentiles throughout the Empire abandoned their own ancient religions and animal

107

sacrifices in the ensuing centuries, they adopted the sacrifice of Jesus as the better substitute.

It is interesting to note in this regard that the last pagan emperor of Rome, Julian (361-3), tried to suppress Christianity and also rebuild the Jewish Temple. He was a pious pagan who truly believed that God desired animal sacrifices. Julian's offer to rebuild the Temple ended when he died in battle. It is not clear to what extent Jews of the time supported his endeavor. Certainly, it was welcomed by at least some, but other Jews had moved on from the Temple.

**The Jewish Answer**

The Judaism of the Pharisees survived the destruction and became Rabbinic Judaism, the Judaism familiar to us. For the Pharisees, the destruction presented an opportunity to fulfill their program, even though they undoubtedly shared in the general Jewish sorrow. The Pharisees had created a way of serving God "as if" they were Temple priests. Their strict observance of ritual purity, which is criticized in the New Testament, was not for them mere legalistic ritualism but a symbolic way of fulfilling the Torah's mandate to be "a kingdom of priests, a holy nation." The Pharisees could not eat tithes, which were reserved for priests, but they could be careful to offer tithes. They could not officiate at sacrifices, but they could maintain the status of ritual purity that was obligatory for officiants. Now that the priests no longer had an institution to support them, the priestly Sadducee party faded away. The Pharisees evolved into the early Rabbis who became the leaders of the Jewish people.

The Rabbis' answer to the question "What replaces sacrifice?" was not so simple and direct as the answer of Christianity. The Rabbis provided a variety of answers.

Jews saw the destruction of the Temple and the loss of Jewish sovereignty as God's punishment for our sins. "On account of our sins we were exiled from our land" it says in the traditional Jewish liturgy. Restoration will come with repentance, patient waiting, divine service, and acceptance of the cup of suffering.

Torah study replaces sacrifice. Sacred study is in itself an offering to God. More specifically, studying the Torah portions of the sacrifices is equal to actually offering the "

Keeping kosher replaces sacrifice. The rabbinic elaboration of kosher laws beyond the biblical requirements established a set of rituals which made the family dinner table "God's little altar." Every meal becomes in Judaism a communion meal with God.

The service of worship replaces sacrifice. The prayers take place at the time of day when the sacrifices were once offered. The prayer-house became, like the family dinner table, a *mikdash mu'at*, a "little Temple" in the words of the prophet Ezekiel.

The rites of Yom Kippur, the Day of Atonement, replace sacrifice. If a Jew will fast and pray on this holy day, and repent misdeeds from the heart, all sins are forgiven. Yom Kippur provides atonement for those who observe it and repent sincerely.

Mitzvot replace sacrifice. Jews believe that "God desires obedience and not sacrifice" (ISamuel 15:22). Observance of the 613 commandments of the Torah is the true service of God from the Jewish point of view.

## As Time Went By

Christians debate whether the sacrament of Holy Communion is a symbolic sacrifice or an actual sacrifice. I was once challenged by a Protestant minister, "How can you Jews claim to have atonement when you have no spilling of blood?" To this minister, according to the teachings of his denomination, actual sacrifice is a necessity. The spilling of Jesus' blood

109

provides an atonement for Christians, in his view, an atonement which Jews no longer possess because Jews do not spill blood upon the altar.

One may respond to this challenge in a number of ways. The term "blood sacrifice" used by some Christians does not ever appear in the Hebrew Bible. The blood of sacrificial animals was dashed against the side of the altar to be drained away, in respect to the animal's soul. Blood was not offered on top of the altar. To Jews it is the offering and service, not the actual blood, which provides atonement. Atonement, for Jews, is accessed post-sacrifice in the manner we have described above. This answer satisfies ourselves, but not those who believe that atonement requires the spilling of blood.

As time went by most Jews and Christians came to see sacrifice as symbolic. By the Middle Ages no one had sacrificed for a thousand years, and the idea of actually offering up an animal to God was not so appealing. Jews and Christians alike had become used to serving God through the rites of worship and the other observances of their own religion.

One strand of Jewish thought, developed by Maimonides and Isaac Abravanel, is that God never wanted sacrifices in the first place. God commanded sacrifices as a concession to the limited understanding of the ancient Israelites, who were accustomed to the religious practices of their neighbors. Once God had taught the people the "service of the heart" which is the true divine service, God took away the Temple. The destruction of the Temple is seen not as a punishment for Israel's sins but as a fulfillment of God's plan.

Another strand of Jewish thought, represented by the Zohar, holds that the sacrifices are eternally dear to God. The Jewish people were never so close to God as when King Solomon's Temple stood. In the messianic times of the future the sacrifices will be restored. There are also Christians who believe that Jews must restore animal sacrifice in order to bring about the Second Coming of Christ. Most Jews and Christians, however, are not at all troubled that the beautiful Muslim Shrine of Omar now stands on the spot where the Temple once stood. The Shrine of Omar has lasted longer than both of the Jewish Temples. The Muslim guardians of the Temple Mount keep a close watch against those few Jews or Christians who may approach the Temple Mount with plans to destroy the Shrine of Omar to make way for the rebuilding of the Temple.

In summary, Christianity and Judaism may be seen as two differing responses to the question, "What replaces sacrifice?" One answer became the religion of the Jewish people, while another answer became the basis of a world religion adopted by many nations.

# CHAPTER THIRTEEN: HOLY DAYS - SABBATH, LORD'S DAY AND HOLIDAYS

## Sabbath and Lord's Day

St. Paul, the founder of Gentile Christianity, told Christians that they did not have to observe the commandments of the Torah, with the exception of the Ten Commandments. As the Ten Commandments include the observance of the Sabbath day, Paul intended the Sabbath to be an aspect of Christian life for Gentile Christians as well as Jews.

Gentile Christianity eliminated the rituals of circumcision and of keeping kosher, aspects of Judaism which were unattractive to Gentiles and were impediments to their conversion. Sabbath, on the other hand, was much admired among Gentiles in the Roman Empire. There were many Gentiles at that time who worshiped the one God as taught by Judaism, but did not observe all the laws of Judaism nor join the Jewish people. These Gentiles were known as God-fearers. The God-fearers were a prime target audience for the missionaries of early Christianity. Many God-fearers observed the Sabbath day of rest.

Over the course of the first few Christian centuries the Christian day of rest was transferred from the seventh day of the week, Saturday, to the first day of the week, Sunday. A religious reason was given for this. Jesus was crucified on a Friday. He died on the cross and was buried that same day. According to Christian belief, Jesus rose from the dead on the third day, which was a Sunday. Christians celebrate Sunday as the Lord's Day, the day that Jesus overcame death and mortality through his resurrection to take his place in Heaven.

There was probably a practical reason as well for the change of days. We are used to living in a society where Christianity is the accepted norm and Jews must struggle to differentiate themselves. In the early Christian centuries that situation was reversed. The whole world knew about the Jews, but they did not know who these Christians were. Christians had a difficult time differentiating themselves, to express to the world that they were not just some kind of Jews but a separate religion with its own beliefs. Having a day of rest on a different day allowed Christians to differentiate themselves. In a similar vein, when Islam arose the Muslims chose Friday as their holy day, claiming a day that was not yet taken by others.

Although the Christians selected a different day, they retained the Jewish concept of the seven-day week. Christians did not change the days of the week. Christians agree with Jews that Sunday is the first day of the week while Saturday, the Sabbath, is the seventh day. Christian calendars start with Sunday on the far left and end with Saturday on the far right.

Sunday, the Lord's Day, is the day when Christians gather for their primary worship service of the week. The Lord's Day is not, however, a day of strict rest as is the Jewish Sabbath.

Because the switch from Saturday to Sunday is not Scriptural and happened by circumstance, there are some Christians who observe the Sabbath day. Seventh Day Adventists are the best known of this group in America. The vast majority of the world's Christians observe Sunday.

Christians were careful to distinguish the Lord's Day from the Jewish Sabbath. An exception to this general rule is certain Protestant sects, including the Puritans who settled North America. These Christian groups called Sunday "the Sabbath", which is still a common practice in American English. The American Puritan Sabbath was a day of rest as it is for the Jews. Unlike the celebratory character of the Jewish Shabbat, the American Sunday Sabbath was a day for critical self-examination. One was expected to spend the day considering one's sinfulness and how one could improve one's own character. When the Sunday School movement began in the 1840's the purpose was not only to improve Christian education but also to make Sunday more entertaining for children who were bored by a day of stillness and introspection. The American Jewish Sunday School was innovated by Rebecca Gratz of Philadelphia based upon this Protestant model. The Protestant Sunday school curriculum consisted of a catechism – a list of required beliefs – and Bible stories. Rebecca Gratz followed a similar model for the Jewish Sunday school.

The Twentieth Century brought us the five-day work week. Until that time most people worked six days a week. It was common in 19th Century America that workers who went to church on Sunday morning were given off Saturday afternoon by their employers. This was a mighty incentive to worship. One impediment to Jewish immigration to America is that Jews found it easy to observe Shabbat in Europe, but in America Jews who were not self employed had to work on Saturday. Ironically, Jews had more religious freedom in oppressive Europe than in free America. The Friday evening worship service, taken for granted by so many American Jews, was an innovation by Rabbi Isaac Mayer Wise in submission to the reality that American Jews worked on Saturday and were not available for traditional Sabbath morning worship.

Through most of history, the fact that Jews took off on Saturday and Christians took off on Sunday was a barrier to social mixing. This was a major factor in Christian-Jewish relations.

**Easter and the Easter Season**

The primary Christian holiday is Easter. Easter celebrates the resurrection of Jesus, his rise from the grave on the third day after his burial. Jesus was arrested in Jerusalem, executed and buried around Passover time. Jesus was in Jerusalem for the pilgrimage. According to the Synoptic Gospels, Jesus was arrested on Passover night, after celebrating the holiday with his disciples in what we would call a seder meal. (The seder as we know had not yet come into being, but there must have been a sort of proto-seder in Jesus' time. The main event of Passover while the Temple stood was the eating of the Passover lamb sacrifice.) According to the Gospel of John, Jesus was arrested the night before Passover and he died on the eve of Passover, at the time that the Passover lambs are sacrificed. The difference between John and the other Gospels is based not on historical memory but on different views of the symbolic meaning of Jesus' death. John's chronology identifies Jesus with the Paschal Lamb. Either way, Easter represents a Christian new understanding of the Jewish observance of Passover.

The date of Easter is set relative to the Jewish calendar, not the Gregorian or Julian calendars which are used, respectively, by Western and Eastern Christians. Passover generally falls on the first full moon after the Spring Equinox – not always, due to the vagaries of the Jewish calendar. Easter falls on the first Sunday after the full moon of the Spring Equinox, except it comes on the following Sunday if the first Sunday would fall on the first day of Passover. Easter was moved away from Passover for purposes of differentiation.

Easter is the holiest day of the year for religious Christians. The worship service is more extensive than on other Sundays. Cultural customs like the Easter bunny and Easter eggs are not directly related to the holiday. Christians eat eggs on Easter for the same reason Jews eat eggs on Passover, a reason which has been obscured by modern methods of egg production. The original reason is that chickens lay more eggs in the Spring, so they are more generally available.

Easter is preceded by Holy Week. A highlight of Holy Week is Good Friday, the day on which Jesus was crucified. We are saddened to admit that for centuries the standard sermon topic for Good Friday was against the faithless Jews. Jews would hide in their homes on Good Friday for fear of anti-Jewish riots that occurred when the worshipers came out of church inflamed with angry passion. We are happy that with the positive transformations that have taken place since the 1960's the annual denunciation of the "perfidious Jews" is no longer usual.

The forty days prior to Easter are known as Lent. This is the penitential period in Christianity. It could be compared to the Ten Days of Repentance between Rosh Hashanah and Yom Kippur, or the Muslim fast of Ramadan. Lent is a season marked by fasting, in our times reserved for Catholics to Ash Wednesday and Fridays. Fasting means two small meals and one regular meal, with no eating between meals. In addition, Catholics refrain from eating meat on Lenten Fridays. That is why it is common to see fish specials on the menu in restaurants on Friday. The day before Lent is "Fat Tuesday", the last day when meat can be eaten before the Lenten fast. Fat Tuesday – Mardi Gras – is celebrated in a festive way. This can be compared to the Jewish festival of Purim, which comes around the same time of year and which is also celebrated with costumes, eating and drinking. The word carnival comes from the Latin *carne vale* – "goodbye to meat." The first day of Lent is Ash Wednesday. Religious Christians of many denominations attend church on that day and receive a cross of ash on their forehead, which they keep all day as a penitential practice. It is interesting to note that when pious Jews of old observed *Tikun Hatzot*, the midnight penitential service, they also placed ashes on their forehead.

## Christmas

Sunday worship and Easter are the primary observances of Christianity. There are many other feast days that fill the Christian calendar, especially in Catholic and Orthodox Christianity. Christmas is one such feast day. It is the feast of St. Nicholas, and it is the day on which Christians celebrated the Nativity, the birth of Jesus. Christmas is one of the more important days on the Christian calendar, which are called by Catholics the Holy Days of Obligation. A Christian might ask a Jew if a certain Jewish holiday is a holy day of obligation, by which they mean, is this a day on which a Jew must refrain from work?

No one really knows the day of the year when Jesus was born. December 25 was chosen because it was the date of an earlier Roman holiday, the Saturnalia. The Jewish festival of Hannukah was first observed on that same date, the 25th day of the first Winter month (later called Kislev), because that was the date on which the Greek King Antiochus celebrated his holiday, the day he chose to rededicate the Jerusalem Temple to his god. Judah Maccabee and his followers chose that exact day, three years later, for the rededication of the Temple which Jews celebrate as Hannukah. The ancients celebrated the third day after the Winter solstice as a holiday of hope, welcoming the return of longer days and more sunlight. This day symbolizes the first glimmer of hope, a hope fulfilled with the Spring equinox when day overcomes night.

This first glimmer of hope, the return of the light, is represented to Christians by the birth of Jesus, to Jews by the rekindling of the Temple lamp after a dark time in Jewish history. Jews and Christians both celebrate the full moon of Springtime as the fulfillment of hope – represented to Christians by the resurrection of Jesus, to Jews by the Exodus from Egyptian slavery. Jews are often self-conscious about the

117

observance of Hannukah out of fear that they are imitating Christians. Actually, the observances are closely related in theme as well as time of year. It is not accidental that both Christians and Jews observe the winter holiday by lighting lights at the darkest time of year.

Another way that Christmas and Hannukah are related is that both were minor holidays until the Nineteenth Century. Hannukah grew more important with the growth of Zionism, Jewish secular nationalism. Judah Maccabee became an important role model for the Zionist movement. Christmas also grew in importance with the growth of secularism. Christmas was given a boost by two literary phenomena. One was the poem *The Night Before Christmas*, more properly named *A Visit from Saint Nicholas*, written by Clement Clarke Moore and published in 1823. The second literary event is Charles Dickens' story *A Christmas Carol*, published in 1843.

Jews may be curious why a traditional Christmas is Victorian in character, when Jesus was born over 2,000 years ago. The answer is that Christmas as we know it in America was an invention of the Victorian Age. Caroling, gifts for children, the whole focus on family life and friendships, originates in the Nineteenth Century.

As for the gift-giving at Christmas and Hannukah, which many religious people think is overdone – well, America is a relatively wealthy country. In former times Christmas gifts were more humble, while the Jewish custom was to give a few coins to children on the fifth night of Hannukah to spend on whatever they wished. Santa Claus, the symbol of the modern American Christmas, bears little resemblance to the historical St. Nicholas. Santa Claus' red and white outfit originated as a marketing tool for Coca Cola. Santa Claus is certainly much loved by American children and by parents who enjoy the fantasy. Jews have to figure out what to do with their own

118

children during the Christmas season. Envy is only human, and it may help to recognize that it's okay to enjoy and appreciate the beautiful celebration of our neighbors while maintaining our own sense of self. How ironic that the popular songs *White Christmas* and *Rudolph the Red Nosed Reindeer* were both written by Jews!

The Christmas tree was a northern European custom that has spread to virtually all American Christians. It may interest Jews to know that East European Christians had a tree custom which they celebrated in the Springtime. Jews had a parallel custom of putting a decorated evergreen tree in their home on the Festival of Shavuot (Pentecost) until that custom was outlawed by Rabbi Elijah of Vilna in the Eighteenth Century. He suspected a non-Jewish origin for the custom, unsurprisingly. It was after Rabbi Elijah outlawed the tree that Jews began to make paper cut flowers for Shavuot, the *shoshantonet*, a custom that persists into our times.

American Jews struggle with the question of whether a Jew may have a Christmas tree in the home. My opinion is that the tree does not belong in a Jewish home. In a time when many nominal Christians practice very little, seldom attend church, but do have a Christmas tree, the tree becomes more than ever a sign of Christian identification. In a more religious age, the tree may have been of lesser significance in the overall scheme of religious identification. Children who have a tree in their home believe themselves to be Christians. Also, one of the primary messages of Hannukah is that Jews should not assimilate into the religious customs of the majority culture. To be a Maccabee is to proudly hold to one's own traditions.

**Pentecost**

On the fiftieth day after Easter – also, then, on a Sunday – Christians celebrate Pentecost. Pentecost is not much noted in our times, just like the Jewish holiday of Shavuot on which it is

# CHAPTER FOURTEEN: THE CHRISTIAN WORSHIP SERVICE

The prayer service as a way of serving God was invented only once in history, by Jews in the late Second Temple era. The Jewish service and the Christian service are both variations on the prayer service that developed as an adjunct to sacrifice in the Jerusalem Temple. When the sacrifices ended, the worship service was expanded to meet the full worship needs of the Jewish people, while Christians developed their own parallel service.

There are no liturgical (regularly recited) prayers in the Hebrew Bible. The Rabbis of old attributed the composition of the prayers to the men of the Great Assembly, a mythical Jewish congress of 120 Sages that was believed to exist in the late Persian and early Greek era. We have no data to support or contradict this belief. By the time the Temple was destroyed in the year 70CE the prayer service was fairly well developed.

The term liturgy refers to a specific set of words and accompanying rituals that make up a service to God. Judaism and Catholic and Orthodox Christianity are all liturgical religions. Many branches of Protestantism are more free-form, worshiping without set words. Many Evangelical Protestants, when they visit a synagogue, are surprised to discover that Jews pray set words out of a book; they imagine that Jesus' own people would pray more like they do, as the Holy Spirit moves them. The fact is that Judaism and historic Christianity are liturgical religions.

Compared to Christian or Muslim worship, the Jewish liturgy has a lot of words. The two parts of the Jewish service, the Recitation of the Shema and the Amidah or Standing Prayer, with their opening and closing additions, constitute an extended essay that would take a long time to read aloud. The set pieces of Christian and Muslim worship are more concise.

The Mass, as traditional Christian worship is called, can be completed in less than an hour. Eastern Orthodox Christians and some Protestant groups prefer a longer service, sometimes as long as an Orthodox Jewish service of three to four hours. Muslims pray five times a day, but each of those prayers is relatively concise.

Is it Jewishly permissible for a Jew to attend a Christian worship service? Most Orthodox rabbis would probably say that a Jew should attend prayer only in a Jewish synagogue. Through most of history, Jewish Christian and Muslim people would not participate in any worship other than their own denomination. Until recent years Catholics and Protestants would not visit one another's churches, even though they are all Christians.

The contemporary age is one of greater openness. A Jew can learn a lot about our neighbors by attending their worship service. Most American Jews welcome Christians to visit our worship services. In particular, there may be many Christian guests at a bar mitzvah observance. Experience tells me that worship is a human activity; we can not only observe but also appreciate and serve God through all sincere worship. I love to see how other people pray, and I have often felt moved by the worship of Christians. I do not fear that this will undermine my faithfulness to Judaism.

My daughter Elisheva, when she was a girl, asked me if she could attend a Christian worship service to see what they do. I took her to a particular Catholic Church where I had a lot of respect for the priest, Father Jack. Father Jack noticed our presence; he spoke words of welcome to us during the Mass. For the next week Elisheva was a big hero at public school. "Wow, Elisheva!" said her friends, "Father Jack said your name right out loud in church." Could Elisheva even tell her already overawed friends that we all went out after church for pizza?

There are certain rules a Jew should follow in a Christian church out of self-respect and respect for Christianity. A Jew should not kneel in prayer. If all the worshipers are kneeling it is acceptable to remain still in one's seat. A Jew should not say "Amen" to any prayer that is said in the name of Jesus or in the name of the Father, the Son and the Holy Spirit. A Jew should not take Communion, the wafer and wine that symbolize the body and blood of Jesus.

What will you see if you attend a Catholic Mass or Protestant worship service? The service will open with some hymns and some prayers, which may vary from service to service. Usually the congregation will recite the Lord's Prayer and the Nicene Creed or a similar Christian creed. These will be described and explained in a later chapter. A Jew might recognize a few phrases that are also found in Jewish worship, such as the "holy, holy holy…." of Isaiah Chapter 6 which is in the Kedushah prayer, and possible "You shall love the Lord your God with all your heart, with all your soul, and with all your might." which is in the Shema (Deut. 6:5)

There will be a Scriptural reading. Jews read from the different parts of our Bible, the Torah and the Haftarah – Prophets. At one time there was also a reading from the Writings, the third section of the Hebrew Bible, but that custom died out. Christians do readings from the different parts of their Bible. There may be an Old Testament reading, a Gospel reading, and a reading from the Epistles. The reading will be preceded and followed by blessings, as in Jewish worship.

At the heart of the Mass is the ceremony of Communion. Worshipers who are spiritually prepared for Communion line up at the altar, the front of the church, where the priest gives them the wafer and wine which have been blessed and

124

consecrated. The worshipers then file silently back to their seats and take a little time to meditate. In a Protestant church Communion may be less formal. The wafer and wine, or grape juice, may be passed to people in their seats. The minister does not serve as an intermediary like the priest in a Catholic church.

Although the Scriptures are read in both Jewish and Christian worship, the Jewish Scriptural reading is probably better compared to the ritual of Communion in Christian worship. Communion symbolizes the salvational act of Christianity, Jesus' death on the cross, while the Torah service symbolizes the salvational act of Judaism, the giving of the Torah at Mount Sinai. The grand ritual of the Torah service in Jewish worship is not so much to hear the Scriptures recited as to reenact the standing at Mount Sinai, as Communion reenacts for a Christian Jesus' Last Supper and his foretelling of his redemptive self-sacrifice.

Depending on the denomination, a Protestant worship service may be as formal and liturgical as the Catholic Mass, or it may be far less liturgical. Going back to the beginnings of Protestantism in Sixteenth Century Germany, the sermon has been a major aspect of Protestant worship. The sermon often takes up most of the worship hour, with much less emphasis on formal prayer. The Protestant sermon generally includes many biblical references. Reform Jews in Germany in the early Nineteenth Century adopted the sermon, with a lot of protest from more traditional Jews. The sermon has gained acceptance in most American synagogues. In the atmosphere of American religion, the Catholic Church also has found it advisable to include a short sermon in the Mass. This message is often called a homily to distinguish it from the lengthier Protestant sermon.

Many evangelical Protestants, when they visit a synagogue for the first time, are surprised to discover how liturgical Jewish worship is. Jews recite our prayers from a book, which is not what one would expect if one knew about Jews only from reading the Bible. This is one of the ways in which Judaism is not "Old Testament religion." In olden times, when only men attended synagogue worship services, Jewish women prayed freestyle while lighting their Sabbath candles. This form of prayer resembles what one might find in an evangelical Protestant church service.

Jewish worship styles have been influenced by the cultural atmosphere of the Christians or Muslims amongst whom Jews reside. The Orthodox or Conservative service resembles in many ways the lengthy, chanted service of Russian Orthodox Christianity. This is an Eastern European way to worship. The Reform worship service – shorter, in the vernacular, with a sermon – more closely resembles German or American Protestant worship.

Many contemporary Protestant churches have dispensed with most of the traditional prayers and rites. The service may begin with some uplifting rock-style hymns, followed by an inspirational sermon aimed towards helping the worshipers deal with their daily life issues. There may be less of an emphasis on salvation of the soul, and certainly less on the condemnation of sin, than one would have heard in earlier times in a Protestant church. Instead, the message is about faith as an aid to living a better life. One might see a Jewish parallel to this trend in the Jewish Renewal service with its focus on the uplifting music of Shlomo Carlebach and Debbie Friedman.

# CHAPTER FIFTEEN: PRIESTS, MINISTERS AND RABBIS

## The Temple Priesthood

In ancient Judaism the religious leaders were hereditary priests. The priests were a caste of the Jewish people. They traced their ancestry to Aaron, the brother of Moses. The Hebrew word for a priest is *cohen*. Many Jews of the last name Cohen are descended from the ancient priesthood. The priests did not work as farmers. They and their families lived from the sacrificial donations of the Jewish people. Priests served as the masters of sacrifice in the Holy Temple in Jerusalem. When people made a sacrifice part of it went to the priests. The "most holy" sacrifices were eaten by priests in the Temple precinct. The ordinary holy sacrifices were eaten by the families of the priests in their homes.

There was a lower order of the priesthood known as Levites. The Levites traced their ancestry to the ancient tribe of Levi, the tribe to which Moses and Aaron belonged. The Levites could not officiate at sacrifices but they fulfilled lower functions at the Holy Temple, such as standing guard and singing in the Temple choir. The Levites were supported by a dedicated tithe.

The High Priest presided over the Temple and also was, for centuries, the national leader of the Jewish people. As we saw in an earlier chapter, later high priests were of questionable authority. In response to this lack of authority challengers arose for religious and political leadership of the Jewish people. This set the stage for new types of religious leader to arise after the destruction of Holy Temple by the Romans in the year 70. After the destruction, the hereditary priests lost the institution which supported their leadership. The priests retained an exalted status which diminished only gradually through the centuries, but the priests now had to work for a living like everyone else. The two religions which arose after the destruction of the Holy Temple, Rabbinical Judaism and Christianity, each established their own new type of religious leader.

## Rabbis

After the destruction of the Temple, the Jewish people were led by a new type of leader called a rabbi. The rabbis seem to have evolved from the Temple era sect of Pharisees. The unique and fateful decision of the Jews is that they would be led by scholars of Torah. A rabbi was distinguished by knowledge of the Scriptures and, even more so, by knowledge of the oral traditions of how to live by the Scriptures. By virtue of education, a rabbi had the ability to derive new laws and rules as needed, consistent with the accepted patterns of interpretation. Unlike the priesthood, the rabbinate was not hereditary. One became a rabbi by becoming a disciple of a rabbi. One learned from the master's teachings and absorbed the life lessons of the master's own life. Some rabbis established schools for the education of future rabbis. Some members of the priesthood became rabbis, but their priestly heritage was irrelevant to their position. What counted was scholarship, knowledge of the traditions, and the ability to interpret Scriptures. The word "rabbi" means "master", deriving from the master-disciple relationship.

Did Jesus' followers address him as "rabbi"? Possibly, but in the time of Jesus, "rabbi" was not yet a formal title. If Jesus was called "rabbi" it did not mean that he was a scholar of Torah, but that his disciples addressed him with respect.

Christian priests and ministers mostly serve a particular church. Rabbis in America typically serve a synagogue, parallel to Christian models of religious organization. The congregational model of the rabbinate is only two centuries old at most. Rabbis in the ancient world were found not in the *beit knesset,* the synagogue, but in the *beit midrash*, the study house. Until modern times, rabbis were hired and appointed by Jewish communities, to serve as leaders, teachers and judges. The chief rabbi of a community would attend the main synagogue but not to lead the worship, which was led by lay people or hired cantors. The rabbi would typically teach a short lesson after the daily morning worship before the folk went off to work. The chief rabbi of a community spent most of his day studying, setting an example of an exalted Jewish life for the people. The congregational rather than communal model of religious leadership is established in America by the First Amendment, which affirms the sovereignty of each individual congregation.

The rabbi did not serve a pastoral role, though people came to the rabbi for advice and for legal judgments. People also believed in the sacred power of rabbis, and people came to them for magical amulets. Christians also came to rabbis for amulets, often to the annoyance of Church leaders. In the Eighteenth Century the new Hasidic movement of Judaism created a new type of Jewish leader called a rebbe. The rebbe may have been a scholar, but he functioned primarily as a pastor and spiritual leader to his followers. The Hasidic movement arose around the same time as evangelical Christianity, in the mid 1700's, and has many parallels. As southern Germany and southern Poland are contiguous, there may have been mutual influences. For a rebbe, his intimacy with God and his pastoral care for his followers were more important than his level of scholarship.

**Priests**

The earliest rabbis, after the year 70, competed with the still powerful priesthood for leadership of the Jewish community. The contrast between priests and rabbis became an important aspect of Judaism. Rabbis were defined not only by what they were but also by what they were not – priests.

The conflict of priests and rabbis was not relevant in Gentile Christianity. In Christianity the Church developed its own ideal of the priesthood. The Christian priest has a kind of continuity with the ancient Temple priesthood. The priest presides over the Mass, the worship service, which is seen as a form of Temple sacrifice. The priest leads from the altar, parallel to the altar of the Jerusalem Temple.

Temple sacrifice was a form of religious ritual which scholars of religion call a sacrament. A sacrament is a ritual which is automatically effective to transform spiritual reality when it is performed in the correct manner by an authorized person. When an ancient Jew brought a sacrifice of atonement to the Temple and the cohen performed the sacrifice in the correct manner, divine forgiveness of sin was the automatic result. The rabbis eliminated sacraments from Judaism. Any Jewish rite can be performed by any Jew. What matters is not correct performance or authorized officiation but *kavannah*, correct intention. A similar debate about sacrament vs. intention arose in Christendom in the Protestant Reformation in the Sixteenth Century.

The rites of Christianity are historically understood as sacraments. Only an ordained priest may preside at the altar during the most sacred parts of the Mass, just as only a Temple priest could enter the inner court of the Jerusalem Temple. Only an ordained Christian priest could administer to the people the sacraments of Baptism, Reconciliation (Confession), Eucharist (Mass) and Anointing of the Sick (Last Rites).

The Christian Church established a hierarchy of religious leadership parallel to the secular hierarchy of the Roman Empire. Each small region, or parish, had a church presided over by a priest. A larger region, a diocese, containing a

number of parishes, was presided over by a bishop. At a higher
level, presiding in the largest and most important cities, was an
archbishop. Certain bishops were appointed as Cardinals to be
the highest council of the Caatholic Church, under the
leadership of the Bishop of Rome, the Pope.

Most of the world's Christians were united into one great
Church for a millennium. In the year 1054 the Church divided
over the leadership of the Bishop of Rome. This division is
called the Great Schism. Western Christians accepted the
ultimate authority of the Pope. They are called Catholic
Christians. Eastern Christians denied the ultimate authority of
the Pope. They accepted the highest authority of regional
archbishops called Patriarchs. These Christians are called
Eastern Orthodox Christians. In Russia, Eastern Europe and the
Middle East most Christians are Orthodox. In Central and
Western Europe and the Americas and Africa most Christians
are Catholic or Protestant. The Protestants broke away from the
Catholic Church in the Sixteenth Century. Some of the earlier
Protestant churches like Anglicans and Lutherans remained
closer to the ideas of Catholicism, while other Protestant
groups moved farther from Catholicism in numerous ways.
The Poles are unique among Slavic peoples in being Catholic
rather than Orthodox, a matter which raised controversies and
even led to wars in Polish-Ukrainian-Russian relations. There
has been violent conflict in our own times between Catholic
Croatians and Orthodox Serbians in the former Yugoslavia.

Priests preside over the church and administer the sacraments
in both Catholic and Orthodox Christianity. To become a
priest, one must be ordained by a bishop. Bishops must be
appointed by the Pope or Patriarch. According to Christian
tradition the line of ordination goes all the way back to Jesus.
Jesus ordained his disciple Peter to establish the Church. Peter
became the first bishop of Rome, the first Pope. Jews believe
that rabbinic ordination goes back to Moses, who ordained his

disciple Joshua. According to Jewish belief the line of ordination was broken in the time of Roman persecutions. Since that time rabbinic ordination is only symbolic. Catholic and Orthodox Christians see their priests as having a religious authority that goes back to the very foundation of their religion.

There are also non-ordained religious leaders in Catholic and Orthodox Christianity. These include monks and nuns, who dedicate their lives to the Church, and deacons, who assist in the functions of the church service but may not administer sacraments on their own authority. Monks and nuns often lived in cloistered communities, abbeys and convents. A distinguishing feature of Judaism, in contrast to Christianity and many other religions, is the absence of such communities. A rough equivalent is that many young Jewish men would spend a number of years as full-time students of Torah, living in the yeshiva academy without possessions or employment. But then the young Jew would go on to marriage, family and work, while monks and nuns give their entire life to the Church.

Christian priests may come from any family and background. They may be scholars, but that is not a requirement. Upon ordination the priest takes vows. The priest vows obedience to the Church. There is an optional vow of poverty. The vow of celibacy – never to marry – was once optional but later became a requirement for Catholic priests. Orthodox priests may marry but if their wife dies, they may not re-marry. Some Catholic priests belong to an order of priests, like the Jesuits or the Paulists. These priests owe their immediate loyalty not to the local bishop but to the leaders of their order. Orders might serve a dedicated function, such as scholarship or mission. Members of a priestly order vow to live by the holy rules established and exemplified by the founder, such as Saint Francis for the Franciscans.

The Catholic priest is the highest leader of his church. He is responsible for the financial security as well as the religious practices and the content of preaching of his church. He is answerable to the bishop for his performance. By contrast, rabbis are usually subject to the authority of a synagogue board of trustees, which reflects the descent of the American synagogue from the prior communal model of Jewish organization. Priests are appointed by the bishop, and serve at his discretion, while rabbis are hired and serve at the will of the synagogue trustees. In premodern times the rabbi was recognized as the *mara d'atra*, the highest authority in his community, but if the elected leaders of the community were displeased with the rabbi's rulings they could fire him and hire a different rabbi.

In recent decades many women have become rabbis in the liberal branches of American Judaism, and women have become ministers in the liberal branches of Protestantism. There are no women priests. It is not for me to say why this is so, but Catholics often point out that in the line of ordination that goes back to Jesus there has never been a woman. We also note that a decision to ordain women to the priesthood would have to be made by the worldwide Catholic Church, under the Pope. Socially conservative Catholics predominate in many countries more than in America.

American Jews are for the most part familiar with Catholic Christianity but not so much with Eastern Orthodox Christianity. The majority of American Jews came to America from Eastern Europe. If they came from Ukraine or Russia, they came from places where Orthodox Christianity predominated. This is culturally significant in a way that few Jews are aware of. While traditional Jewish worship is different in style and time sense from the Protestant-style worship of Reform Jews, it is similar to the worship style of Orthodox Christians. It may also be culturally significant that only

Orthodox Jews and Orthodox Christians, out of all the religious sects in America, continue to worship in the ancient language of their liturgy and have not made the switch to English. The Catholic Church in America allowed for the Mass to be recited in the vernacular – English or sometimes Spanish in the USA - after the Second Vatican Council, though there are still old-style Catholics who prefer the Latin Mass. The Catholic Church in America has attempted to accomodate those Catholics by providing the Latin Mass in some churches. It could be that the American Jewish penchant for praying in Hebrew is not just an aspect of Jewishness but also an aspect of immigration from Eastern Europe.

**Protestant Ministers**

The Protestant movement of Christianity began in 1517. According to legend, the young priest Martin Luther nailed his 95 Theses to the church door of Wittenburg Castle in Germany on October 31 of that year. The 95 Theses were complaints against alleged corrupt practices that had become common in the Roman Catholic Church. What began as a protest movement within the Church soon became a movement to separate from the Church. In part this was because the secular rulers of Northern Europe were prepared to break from the spiritual rule of Rome and establish nationally based Christian Churches.

The Protestant movement fractured as different leaders established their own Protestant denominations based on their separate visions of a purified Christianity. Lutherans follow the teachings of Martin Luther. Presbyterians, Dutch Reformed and others follow the teachings of John Calvin and are called Calvinists. The Methodists follow the teachings of John Wesley, who branched out from the Church of England. There are various types of Baptists. To trace the entire evolution of Protestantism is beyond the scope of this book. Most

Protestants share certain characteristics in their expression of Christianity. The Episcopal Church has a separate history. The Church of England broke away from the Pope over the issue of divorce but were not part of the Protestant revolution. Though counted amongst Protestants, Episcopalians are in some ways non-Roman Catholics. Ordained Protestant religious leaders are called ministers, not priests, but Episcopalian clergy, who are allowed to marry, are still called priests. Episcopalians are American members of the Church of England, the Anglican Communion.

For many years Europe was torn by wars between Protestant and Catholic powers. Some of these wars were between nations, others were civil wars. Ultimately Catholics and Protestants had to learn to live together, for the wars were interminable and indeterminate and the people could not endure them. Central and Western Europe developed a new cultural expression we call "religion". Religion is a personal expression of faith that one could hold in one's heart and mind while participating in secular civil society. The evolution of "religion" is important for Judaism in America and in the Western world. Religion permitted Jews to participate in civil society when the political revolutions of the Enlightenment era made that possible beginning in the late 18th Century. Jews who wished to participate in civil society after the French Revolution, especially in Germany and the United States, re-cast Judaism as a religion. Some would argue that Judaism, as the way of life of a nation, does not fit well into the Christian concept of religion, but it has enabled Jews to thrive in secular societies. American Jews are often puzzled that Israelis do not "get" the American concept of Jewish religion. This is largely because most Israelis come from countries where the Western and Central European concept of "religion" never took hold. Jews from the Russian Empire, and Jews from Arab lands, came to Israel from places where "religion" was unknown, and one's faith was part and parcel of one's total way of life.

The Protestant Reformation, as it is called, was in part a rebellion against priestly religion. In that regard it has interesting parallels to the rabbinic revolution against the Temple priesthood 1,500 years earlier. Protestant ministers are not called priests because they do not stand as intermediaries between God and the people as priests do. Protestants partly or fully eliminated sacraments, which as we have discussed are rituals which are automatically effective when performed in the right way by authorized persons. Protestants see Christian rites as expressions of a personal relationship with God. A Protestant does not need to confess to a minister before taking Communion. To use a Jewish term, Christian rites in Protestantism require *kavannah*, intention, more than correct performance.

Some Protestants, including Lutherans and Calvinists, recognize the sacraments of baptism and communion, which they see as Scripturally based. The division between Catholics and Protestants concerning sacraments is not absolute.

Baptism is a good example of the distinction between sacramental and non-sacramental rites. In Catholic Christianity babies were baptized into the Church as soon as possible after birth, in order to protect their souls in the salvation of Christ. Many Protestants saw this form of baptism as not meaningful because the baby has no intention to become a Christian. These Protestants replaced infant baptism with baptism after entering the age of reason. In Baptist Christianity, a Christian is baptized only when he or she has chosen to give themselves to Christ, which could take place at any point in life. These Protestants often practice full immersion, like the Jewish mikvah immersion, rather than sprinkling with holy water that has been blessed by a priest, as in the Catholic Church. In our times many Protestant Christians go to the Jordan River in Israel, to be baptized where John the Baptist immersed Jesus.

Church law prohibited the baptizing of Jews against their will. Nevertheless, it sometimes happened, as when the entire Jewish population of Portugal were forcibly baptized in 1497. The Jews of Portugal appealed to the Pope. The Pope responded that while the baptism was illegally performed, it is nevertheless effective as a sacrament. The Jews of Portugal were now Christians and subject to the Inquisition if they did not live as faithful Christians.

Protestant ministers, like Catholic priests, lead worship in a Christian church, but their role is different. The priest administers the sacraments of the Church. The primary role of the Protestant minister is to preach the word of God as inspired by the Holy Spirit.

Prior to the Protestant Reformation, within the Catholic Church only priests were permitted to read the Bible. As Protestantism is in part a protest against priestly authority, it became important for every Protestant Christian to read the Bible for themselves. Martin Luther translated the Bible into the German language to make it accessible to the masses. The King James Bible in English was published not long after, in 1611. Jews may wonder why there are no earlier Bible translations for Christians. The answer is that in pre-Protestant Christianity the Bible was studied only by priests, who were trained to read the original Greek or the Vulgate, the official Latin translation created by St. Jerome in the Fourth Century.

Bible reading is a uniquely Protestant activity. Jews learned the Bible in Hebrew in their elementary education, but thereafter focused their study on Talmud and its related literature. Catholic priests had a parallel course of study in the writings of the Church Fathers and later Church teachings as they evolved through the centuries. Protestants attempted to go back to the beginning of Christianity by bypassing later Christian thought and going right to the Bible. Protestants read the Jewish Bible, their Old Testament, as well as the Christian New Testament. Protestants are often more conversant with Israelite history than are Jews. Bible reading is also largely responsible for Protestant support for Zionism. Many English Christians who helped advance Zionism in its formative stages, like Balfour and Wingate, were ardent Bible readers.

Some American Protestants think of Jews as being more like them than we are like Catholics, seeing that Jews and Protestants are people of the Bible. This is not exactly true, as the Oral Torah gives Jews an ongoing tradition which is similar to the Church tradition of the Catholics. It does benefit us Jews to be thought of as the people of the Bible. It would be nice if Bible readers realized that we are no longer tribal, and we have not offered an animal sacrifice for two thousand years now. We have not walked out of the pages of ancient history. Jews need to educate Bible readers out of that misunderstanding gently and with affection.

When Jews exited the walled-in ghettos of German cities in the 18th Century we entered a world which was primarily Protestant. Jews who wanted to modernize Judaism and make it more like the religion of their neighbors introduced preaching into the synagogue. The Reform Jews saw this as culturally desirable and also as necessary to keep Jews Jewish now that they were attending public schools and getting less Jewish education. Traditional Orthodox Jews objected to turning rabbis into preachers. The traditional rabbi preached only twice a year, to teach the laws of repentance before Yom Kippur and to teach the laws of Passover observance. The Reformers recruited the Jewish scholar Leopold Zunz, who in 1845 published a historical study proving that the Jews had actually invented the sermon in the ancient synagogue. This was factually true but somewhat disingenuous as the Jewish reformers were clearly following Protestant models.

In contemporary America the Catholic Church has also found it advisable to have priests give a homily at Sunday Mass. This may be an adjustment to living in a predominantly Protestant nation. It may be that the Catholic Church has found that in this secular age the people need some words of inspiration. Religious devotion can no longer be taken for granted. In Orthodox synagogues, also, there may now be a sermon.

In his New Testament Epistles, Saint Paul emphasizes the saving value of faith above good deeds, which he called "works". Despite the teachings of Paul, as Christianity became the religion of nations and empires the Church found it necessary to establish behavioral objectives for Christian living. The Church developed its own body of laws. The Protestant Reformation placed a new focus on the teachings of Paul. Faith alone brings salvation. This focus on salvation through faith is the basis for the renowned Protestant Work Ethic. A Christian who is saved by faith alone, or even by predetermined divine choice (Predestination), is identifiable by his or her righteous deeds. The saved Christian behaves in a way that demonstrates that he or she is among God's elect. Paradoxically, a focus on faith and predestination inspired American Protestants to work harder and longer than people ever had in the past.

The ministers of some Protestant denominations dress in the identifiable clothing of Christian clergy, the collar. There may be a stylistic difference between the Roman collar and the Protestant collar, but not such as a Jew would notice. The Roman Catholic priest will usually wear black, while a Protestant minister may wear a colorful shirt with a clergy collar. The ministers of Protestant denominations which define themselves as "not Catholic" may often be seen wearing a tan suit. This style of dress is common with television preachers. The tan suit says without words, "not a priest." Some contemporary pastors may dress in a more casual style, dispensing with all formality, and Catholic priests in our time may go about in regular clothing on a daily basis. Very few nuns in our times wear the habit we stereotypically think of. Many nuns, like priests and ministers of today, find that they connect better with the flock by dressing in contemporary style.

**Conclusion**

A priest, a minister and a rabbi go to the golf course. The golf pro says to them, "Hey, what is this – the beginning of a joke?"

The religious leaders of all religions have certain things in common. They all must be faithful shepherds guiding their flock while providing comfort and hope. There are differences of focus and emphasis in different religions. The traditional rabbi is first and foremost a scholar of Torah, tradition and law. The Catholic priest first and foremost administers the saving sacraments of the Church. The Protestant minister is first and foremost a preacher of God's Word.

# CHAPTER SIXTEEN: FUNDAMENTALISM

American Protestants can be roughly divided into two groups –
liberal Protestants and Fundamentalists. In contemporary
American English we use the term Fundamentalist to describe
traditionalist religious opponents of contemporary culture in
any religion. Assemblies of God Protestants, ultra-Orthodox
Jews, and Wahabi Muslims are all characterized as
Fundamentalists. These groups do have a great deal in
common. Technically, the term Fundamentalist refers to a
movement of 19th Century Protestantism that confirms a set of
beliefs known as the Fundaments. The essence of Christian
Fundamentalism is the belief in the literal truth and inerrancy
of the Bible. Fundamentalists believe that the Bible says only
one thing, that this one thing is exactly what the words seem to
be saying, and that this message is factually true. The Bible can
never be wrong.

The beliefs of Fundamentalist Christianity conflict with the
natural sciences. The Theory of Evolution, based on scientific
evidence, suggests that the universe is about 14 billion years
old, the planet Earth is about 5 billion years old, and the human
species evolved from other life forms. Fundamentalist
Christians believe that the universe was created by God
somewhat less than six thousand years ago, exactly as it is
today, with humankind as the crown of Creation.

The principles of Fundamentalism are foreign to Judaism, even
ultra-Orthodox Judaism. Literalism is not a part of Judaism.
Jewish tradition teaches (Numbers Rabbah) that every verse
and phrase in the Bible has seventy different interpretations, all
of which are true in some sense, even though they may
contradict one another. The greatest Jewish Scripture
commentator, Rashi (11th Century France) often says of a
verse, "This verse cries out, 'Interpret me.'" (*Darsheni!*) When
Jews study Torah they enjoy learning the conflicting

interpretations of Rashi, Ibn Ezra and Nahmanides, which are printed around the page of the biblical text. In contrast, Fundamentalist Christians prefer to hear the words of a trusted preacher who will tell them exactly what the Bible is saying. It may seem strange to a Jew to hear a Fundamentalist friend say that "The snake in the Garden of Eden story is literally Satan." Is that really literalism? It is to our friend.

Jewish Fundamentalism – ultra-Orthodoxy – is in conflict with the science of history rather than the natural sciences. With few exceptions, Orthodox Jews are not challenged by the scientific theory of Evolution, which is remarkably consistent with Medieval Kabbalistic speculation about the cosmos. Jewish Fundamentalists defend the belief that God gave the whole Torah to Moses at Mount Sinai, including the laws and rules that would be set down 1,500 years later in the Talmud. Historical analysis suggests that the text of the Torah went through its own evolution and reached its final form centuries after the time of Moses. Christian Fundamentalism was challenged by the famous Scopes Monkey Trial (1925), in which the Theory of Evolution took center stage. Orthodox Fundamentalism is challenged by the findings of historical study and archeology more than by the discoveries of science.

Many Fundamentalist Christians support the State of Israel because they believe it is a necessary prerequisite to the Second Coming of Christ, which will be preceded by a world war in which most Jews will die. The remaining Jews will be converted to Christianity at the Second Coming. The peculiar role of the Jews in Christian Fundamentalist apocalyptic thought is well represented in the popular *Left Behind* series of novels by Tim LaHaye and Jerry B. Jenkins. Some Jews reject Fundamentalist support for Israel because of its dire future vision for Jews, while other Jews welcome Fundamentalist support because it is of practical help to Jews in the here and

142

now, while Jews can agree to disagree about the Second Coming scenario.

Liberal Protestants are more likely to validate Judaism as a religion, but they are also more likely to harshly judge the State of Israel in its conflict with the Palestinians. This presents a challenge to Jews. Who is our better friend – liberal Protestants who validate our religion, or Fundamentalist Protestants who validate our national self-determination? If only we could have both!

The Catholic Church is a big tent. There are Catholics whose political and religious views are closer to those of the Fundamentalists, and others whose views are more like those of the liberal Protestants. Since 1943, when Pope Pius XII issued the encyclical *Divino Afflante Spiritu*, Catholic scholars have been encouraged to use the tools of modern science to study the Bible. This puts the Catholic Church officially outside the Fundamentalist camp.

The historical analysis and scientific critique of the Scriptures has challenged Judaism and Christianity to evolve in their beliefs and teachings to accommodate modernity. The scientific revolution presents a unique challenge to Muslims, who mostly did not participate in the 18th and 19th Century European Enlightenment. What would be the result to Islam if Muslims applied historical analysis to the Koran, which according to Islamic belief was dictated to Mohammed by the angel Gabriel? Muslims must forge their own path to find an accommodation between tradition and modernity.

Secularists often criticize the Catholic Church for having put Galileo under house arrest for his scientific teachings, particularly his demonstration that the planets revolve around the sun and they have their own moons. In fairness to Galileo, he was a devout Catholic, and his opponents in the Vatican were the leading scientists of their day before Galileo came along. Galileo's opponents were defending not Christianity but the scientific theories of Aristotle, which had been accepted by the Church. Galileo's opponents were like tenured professors of today trying to suppress a young physicist's paper at the annual conference because it threatens the older theories upon which their own reputations rest. Human nature has not been transformed by the scientific revolution.

Some forms of Christianity see science and religion as inherently in conflict. If most Jews do not, that is largely due to the influence of Maimonides. The great Medieval rabbi Maimonides (d. 1205) argued that since God is one, truth is one. Since the human mind was created by God, human reason intuits God's single truth. Science and the Bible both have their source in

God and so cannot be contradictory. Human reason must interpret the Bible allegorically to be consistent with scientific understandings in order to maintain the unity of Truth.

Fundamentalism must explain the existence of natural phenomena like fossils, geological strata, and carbon dating, which lead humans into accepting science over a literal reading of the Bible. The usual answer is that the Devil has planted these phenomena in the material world to mislead humankind. This understanding is not possible for Jews, for whom the Devil does not exist. Maimonides insists that human reason is faithful and reliable because its source is in God. We therefore interpret the Bible not literally, but in a way that validates the findings of science so that Truth is one. It is largely due to Maimonides' influence on Judaism that the principles of Fundamentalism have not found a ready home in the Jewish religion. That has not stopped some Jews from relying on traditional Judaism as a bulwark against what they see as a degraded contemporary culture. The belief that the modern world is a threat to cherished traditional values unites

144

Fundamentalists of all religions. Many *Haredi* Jews share with Christian Fundamentalists the view that God is micromanaging the world, overruling the course of nature as required to benefit the faithful.

# CHAPTER SEVENTEEN: IDOLATRY

Judaism prohibits the worship of idols - statues and pictures of gods. Do Jews think of Christians as idol worshipers? Christians would say of themselves that they are definitely not idol worshipers. The three monotheistic religions of Judaism, Christianity and Islam all prohibit idolatry. Jews wonder about Christians because we observe Christians showing reverence to statues and pictures of Jesus, Mary, and the Saints. What is a Jew supposed to think when we see these things?

Our understanding of idolatry is confused by a misunderstanding that arose long ago. The prophet Isaiah mocked the idolatry of the Babylonians by suggesting that idolaters carve a piece of wood or stone into a statue and then pray to that statue as a god. (Isaiah 44:9-20) Isaiah was being funny, but people tend to take Scriptures literally. By this standard no one is an idol worshiper, for no person of any religion believes that the statue he manufactures is an actual god. The worshiper rather believes that the power and spirit of the deity are focused into the statue when it becomes an object of worship. The misunderstanding created by Isaiah gives the idol worshiper a disclaimer, that "since I worship the statue but do not think of it as an actual god I am not an idolater."

Another confusion arose in ancient Judaism concerning idol worship and the worship of other deities. The Ten Commandments opens: I am Ad-nai your God who brought you out of the land of Egypt, the house of bondage; You shall have no other gods beside Me; You shall not make for yourself a sculptured image...." (Ex. 20:2-4) This is the first two commandments. It is not clear in the Hebrew whether the prohibition of other gods belongs to the First Commandment or the Second Commandment. Christians place the prohibition in the First Commandment, which is logical. Jews place the prohibition in the Second Commandment. Idols are thus

146

equated with other gods. This understanding made sense in Greek and Roman times, when Jews were the only monotheists and also the only people to worship God without idols. Idols and other gods were conflated to be one and the same thing. It could be argued, then, from the Jewish understanding, that a statue is not an idol unless it is also polytheistic. This runs contrary to the story of the Golden Calf, which is an idol to God. Nevertheless, to the early rabbinic Jews, idols meant other gods.

The ancient rabbis could be sophisticated in their understanding of what constitutes an idol. When Rabban Johanan ben Zakkai was challenged by a Roman philosopher for attending a bath house despite the presence of a statue of Aphrodite, the rabbi responded that since men walked around in the nude before the statue it clearly was not an object of worship but only a decoration, and therefor not prohibited to Jews. (Babylonian Talmud Avodah Zarah 44b) On the other hand the rabbis could be quite strict. They understood the two-fold prohibition "you shall not worship them nor serve them" to mean that a Jew is prohibited from performing the sacred service of a statue of a god even if he or she does not believe in or genuinely worship that god. Many Jews of today will put a flower in front of a statue of the Buddha when attending a meditation class, arguing that this is not worship, but the rabbis of old would disapprove of this practice as idolatry nonetheless. All of these factors come into play in our Jewish evaluation of Christianity in relation to idols.

Jews are stricter than Christians about what constitutes idolatry, but Muslims are stricter than Jews. Islam prohibits any artistic depictions of a person or creature. Traditional Islamic art is purely geometric and non-representational for this reason.

The mosaic tile floors of some Byzantine era synagogues were preserved for archeologists to find because they were paved over in a later age with plain stones. The mosaics often depict Abraham offering Isaac on the altar, and even Helios driving the disk of the sun across the sky. In one era, these depictions were not thought of as idols. A century of two later Jews did think of these depictions as idols and they paved them over. We can see that it is hard to come to a consensus about what constitutes idolatry.

Jewish law restricts commercial and social interactions with idolaters. These prohibitions were specifically not applied to Christians and Muslims. Christians and Muslims were placed into a separate legal category, not Jews but not idolaters either.

It is commonly mis-stated of Jews that Jewish law permits a Jew to cheat non-Jews in business transactions. That is not a fair assessment. Jewish law does have rules that apply in business only between two Jews; it is common for any legal system to apply some rules only to those living under the same law. In transactions with non-Jews when the Jewish merchant is not constrained by the law the general ethical principle of "sanctification of the Name of God" obligates a Jew to uphold the highest ethical standards in relations with the non-Jewish world so as to bring honor to God. When some Jews do not live up to that standard, it is not because they are Jewish but because they are human, and so subject to the same temptations and failings as every human.

The ambiguous status of Christians under Jewish law was clarified at the Disputation of Paris in 1240. Queen Blanche of France ordered the Jews to provide rabbis to debate the value of the Talmud with a Christian scholar, Nicholas Donin. Donin was a converted Jew who had denounced the Talmud to the French authorities. The Jews were led by the great Rabbi Yehiel. According to the Hebrew transcript of the trial, towards the end of the trial the Queen asked Rabbi Yehiel directly whether Jews consider Christians to be idolaters or worshipers of the One true God. Rabbi Yehiel responded that in the eyes of the Jews, Christians are monotheists and not idolaters. Whether Rabbi Yehiel's response was motived by expedience or genuine belief, it was now part of the public record. Jews had it on the authority of their leading rabbi that Christians are not to be thought of as idol worshipers.

Regardless of the official Jewish position, there can be little doubt that when ordinary Jews observed icons and statues of Jesus and of Mary they associated those depictions with the prohibited idols that the prophets so resoundingly denounced in the Bible. Protestants have been more direct in their judgment of Catholic and Orthodox Christianity. A Protestant cross does not contain a figure of Jesus on it. This is partially a rejection of imagery seen as idolatrous, and partially a focus on the Resurrection as opposed to the Crucifixion. Protestants generally oppose the worship of Mary the mother of Jesus, and would not set up statues of her. Some Protestants actively denounce what they call "Mariolatry." At the same time this does not prevent many Protestants from having paintings of Jesus on the wall in their homes and churches and public places. The depiction of Jesus with straight light brown hair and a sharp aquiline non-Semitic nose is an American Protestant invention. Orthodox Christians love icons, paintings of Christian saints. A group arose which opposed icons as idols. Called the Iconoclasts, they destroyed all the icons they could get their hands on. Eventually the Iconoclasts were overthrown and icon painting was restored. Some of the oldest Orthodox Christian icons in existence are to be found at Santa Katarina monastery at Mount Sinai, which never fell into the hands of the Iconoclasts. We see that within the Christian world there is a lot of debate over what constitutes an idol.

In the Book of Exodus in the Torah, right after the incident of the worship of the Golden Calf, God commands the Israelites to make two cherubim to flank the holy Ark. The cherubim are winged angel figures. The Jewish commentator Rashi asks what is the difference between the Golden Calf and the cherubim? He answers that they are not different at all except that one is prohibited by God and the other is commanded by God.

# CHAPTER EIGHTEEN: RITUAL PURITY AND BAPTISM

In ancient Israel a person who wished to attend a sacrifice or eat sacrificial meat had to be in a state of ritual purity – *tahor*. A person who was not in this state of being was ritually impure – *tamei*. The King James Bible translates these words as "clean" and "unclean" but that is inaccurate. Pure and impure have nothing to do with hygiene and cleanliness. The terms refer only to a ritual status related to sacrifice. Priests who ate sacrifice on a regular basis strove to remain ritually pure at all times. Other Israelites in biblical times probably only concerned themselves about purity laws when they were going to bring a sacrifice.

The primary sources of ritual impurity are contact with the dead, unkosher animals, and certain flows from the sexual organs, including a woman's monthly blood flow. When a person contracted ritual impurity, one had to go through a ritual of purification. Details varied, but purification includes immersion in a mikvah. A mikvah is a pool of living water large enough for complete immersion. Piped water is not living water. Living water is collected rainwater (the usual source in a modern mikvah), a natural spring, a river or lake or the ocean.

In late Second Temple times, the time of Jesus, ritual purity had acquired added spiritual significance. Pharisees attempted to live a priestly life, even though most of them were not priests, in fulfillment of the biblical commandment "You shall be to Me a kingdom of priests and a holy people." (Exodus 19:6) Multitudes of Jews observed the ritual purity laws. One can see the extent to which ritual purity was observed if you go to an antiquities museum in Jerusalem. There you will see plates and drinking cups from the last years of the Temple, carved from basalt. Jews who could afford these used plates and cups carved out of solid rock because, being a natural material, rock was not subject to ritual impurity. Clay plates are objects of human artifice, and so may become impure through contact with unkosher food or the carcass of an impure animal. Archeology also shows that the well-to-do in ancient Jerusalem had a private mikvah in their own basement. Archeologists have unearthed a mikveh at Qumran of the Dead Sea Scrolls community. The mikvah comports with Jewish law as described in the Talmud.

Jesus is depicted in the Gospels as being opposed to the extreme interpretation of the purity laws. Jesus was criticized for dining with people who were not likely to be careful about ritual purity. This scenario is entirely plausible. Jesus may well have opposed what he perceived to be the fad of the times. It is likely that Galilean Jews were not as strict in these matters as Jerusalemites. Reform Judaism in 19th Century Germany and America also took a dim view of ritual purity laws, and these laws are observed today mostly by Orthodox Jews. It is not fair, though, for contemporary Christians to take Jesus' critique of purity laws as a sign that Judaism is a religion of outward ritualism. It is easy for people of any religion or sect to denounce the distinctive identity rituals of other religions and sects. One must experience these rituals from the inside to know what they mean to their adherents and believers. As we have noted, for Pharisees the purity laws were a symbol of their communion with God as a priestly people.

As Christianity became a Gentile religion, Christians eliminated the obligation to observe purity laws. The Book of Acts decrees that the kosher laws of forbidden animals are now null and void (Acts 10). Ritual purity is not relevant in Christianity.

There is one aspect of ritual purity which Christians retained and which is central to the Christian religion. This is the ritual of immersion in water or sprinkling with holy water as a rite of entry into the Christian faith. Christians call this rite of initiation "baptism."

In the time of Jesus there lived a Jewish holy man who Christians call "John the Baptist." John might more accurately be called "John the Mikvah Man", because the immersions that John performed were Jewish. Christians see John and his activities as a kind of proto-Christianity. John lived in the wilderness of Judea by the Jordan River. He lived simply like the biblical prophet Elijah, wearing rough clothing and living off the land on locusts and wild honey. John immersed his visitors in the Jordan River, which served as his mikvah. John saw immersion not just as an act of ritual purity, but as a rite to purify the human soul and effect a transformation of the whole person. People flocked to John, including many residents of Jerusalem, to hear him preach a lesson of renewal and to be immersed by him in the Jordan River.

Jesus' public career began when he went to John at the Jordan River. Jesus went down as a simple carpenter's son from Nazareth in the Galilee. He was immersed by John. Jesus had a vision of God's Holy Spirit as a result of his immersion. He began to wander the Galilee, preaching the imminent coming of God's Kingdom and the need for people to transform their lives in preparation for the Kingdom. A year or two later Jesus went up to Jerusalem, where he was arrested and crucified. In the meantime, John was arrested and beheaded by King Herod Antipas because John had been denouncing him for his incestuous marriage.

Christians see John the Baptist as the forerunner of Jesus Christ. Jews believed that God would send Elijah the Prophet to announce the coming of the Day of God, eventually understood to be the day of the coming of the Messiah. Christians give John the role of Elijah the Prophet and Jesus the role of Messiah. It remained for Christianity to explain

153

why, if Jesus is divine, he would need to be immersed in a ritual of purification. The explanation is that John recognized Jesus' superiority but immersed him nevertheless as an example that "all righteousness must be performed."

Christians believe that baptism washes the soul clean of the taint of Original Sin, the sinfulness which has inhered in humankind since Adam and Eve disobeyed God and ate from the Tree of Knowledge of Good and Evil. An unbaptized soul is destined for eternal damnation, while a baptized soul is destined for Heaven thanks to the saving grace of Jesus Christ. Historically, Christians were anxious to baptize newborns as soon as possible, lest they die unsaved. Babies were brought to church, where their forehead was sprinkled with blessed holy water. New converts to Christianity were likewise baptized. Some Protestants believe that baptism should take place only when a person is old enough to make a personal commitment to Christ. These Protestants generally practice full immersion, after the ancient Jewish manner performed by John, rather than sprinkling. Many such Protestant believers are known as Baptists. Unlike Jewish immersion which is performed in privacy in the nude, so that the body has full contact with the water, Christian immersion takes place while fully clothed in regular clothing or a special robe. Some Protestants may go to a river or lake to perform immersion baptism.

The cult of Mithra, a Persian religion, became very popular in the Roman Empire. New converts to Mithraism were baptized in the blood of a bull, which was sacrificed for the occasion. Christianity adopted the language of Mithraism when they said of newly baptized Christians that they were "washed in the blood of the Lamb", Jesus being the Lamb.

Jews, your Christian friend may be deeply worried for you because you are not baptized. Your friend may believe that regardless of your righteous life and Jewish observance you are

154

destined for Hell because you have not been baptized. Your friend will not be satisfied with your explanation that you are confident your Jewish religion is sufficient to gain you blessing in the afterlife. There's not much one can say in response to your friend's concern. You can acknowledge to yourself that the intention is good and for your sake. Console yourself to know that many Christians in today's world do believe that a Jew can enter Heaven. Sometimes Christians debate amongst themselves whether an unbaptized Jew may enter Heaven and whether God hears the prayer of a Jew. This may be uncomfortable for us but the debate is not really about us; it is a debate between Christians about their own sense of the significance of Christian rites. Are they sufficient, or necessary, for salvation of the soul?

In former times if a Jew was baptized against his or her will that Jew was obligated under Christian law to live as a Christian. We have mentioned that this happened in 1497 to the entire Jewish population of Portugal. In the 1850's an Italian Jewish child was secretly baptized by his nursemaid. When this came to light the child, Edgardo Mortaro, was kidnapped from his family and raised by the Church. He became a priest in adult life. There was an international controversy surrounding this case. During the Holocaust some families rescued Jewish children and raised them as Christians. Some of these children returned to Judaism after the war, while many of them remained faithful to Christianity. One such Jew, Jean-Marie Lustiger, became Archbishop of Paris and a Cardinal of the Catholic Church. There are Jewish legends about a Jewish Pope, a kidnapped child who rose to the papacy and remained secretly loyal to his people. There is no reason to believe that this actually ever happened.

In America, where interfaith marriage is common, the birth of a baby sometimes results in a contest between the grandparents over the religion of the child. The Christian grandparents may be anxious to see the baby baptized, while the Jewish grandparents want to see a circumcision for a boy or a synagogue naming ceremony for a girl. In these cases it is best for the whole family to be included in the decision making, and for everyone to consult with religious leaders whose direction they trust. It should be understood that the choice of a birth ceremony, whether baptism or a Jewish ceremony, is not just an empty ritual but a decision about the religion in which the child will be raised.

In Catholicism and some Protestant denominations a baby who is baptized is appointed a godfather and godmother. These persons have a lifelong responsibility to see that the child is raised as a good Christian. Many American Jews ask a rabbi about godparents for their children. There is no such custom in Judaism. The *kvaterin* who present a baby for circumcision and the *sandek* who holds the baby are honors just for the duration of the ceremony, with no lifelong significance.

Some Christians who practice adult baptism speak of being "born again" in Christ. Jews do not speak in these terms, but a convert to Judaism who goes into the mikvah and emerges as a Jew has a similar exalted experience. Passing through the waters is indeed a new birth on the spiritual plane. I immersed myself in the mikvah of Rabbi Isaac Luria in Zefat, Israel just a few years prior to this writing. This mikvah is a very cold natural spring which has been covered over by a stone bathhouse. Rabbi Isaac Luria introduced ca. 1580 the practice of mikvah immersion for men as a purely spiritual activity, especially on Friday afternoons in preparation for the Sabbath. The Jewish custom of mikvah is to immerse three times. I did the first trio of immersions to get used to the cold, then another trio to think about the historical significance of the place, then a final trio to be spiritually present to the occasion. The person next to me in the changing room said to me as we were drying ourselves "*zeh mashehu*" – "that was really something!" Yes, it was.

# CHAPTER NINETEEN: COMMUNION

Holy Communion, also called the Eucharist, is the most sacred sacrament in Catholic and Orthodox Christianity. In the Eucharist a Christian relives Jesus' self-sacrifice, which is the foundation of his or her own salvation. A Jew may compare this, in terms of religious significance, to the Passover Seder, by virtue of which a Jew may say "I was a slave in Egypt and God saved me from there." Through sacred ritual, historical events become personal experiences. The word communion means to interact on the deepest personal level. In religion, communion brings God and the worshiper into intimate relationship.

Christian Communion is based on the story of Jesus' Last Supper as told in the three Synoptic Gospels. According to these Gospels Jesus' final meal was a Passover dinner, held in the company of his closest disciples in the Garden of Gethsemane in Jerusalem. As told in the Gospel of Matthew:

Now as they were eating, Jesus took bread, and blessed, and broke it, and gave it to the disciples and said, "Take, eat. This is my body." And he took a cup (of wine), and when he had given thanks he gave it to them, saying, "Drink of it, all of you, for this is my blood of the covenant, which is poured out for many for the forgiveness of sins. I tell you I shall not drink again of this fruit of the vine until that day when I drink it new with you in my Father's kingdom." (Matthew 26:26-29)

Based on this passage, Christians at worship eat a piece of matzah and drink a sip of wine, representing the body and blood of Christ. As the term Communion suggests, this act puts the worshiper into an intimate relationship with God.

In Catholic Christianity, the worshiper who wishes to partake of communion must first be baptized as a Catholic or in another Christian denomination which is in communion with the Catholic Church. That person must also partake of the sacrament of Confession to be sure of approaching God in a state of grace and not in a state of sinfulness.

Jewish people are probably aware of Confession from the confession booths that appear in many movies. The booth has private seating for the worshiper and a space for the priest who receives confession, divided by a screen. The penitent may confess anonymously, or face to face. Jewish confession is communal ("For the sin which we have sinned against You, O God, we ask for forgiveness.) and between the worshipers and God. Catholic confession is individual and requires a priest as an intermediary. The priest may recommend prayers and acts of penance. In the name of God, the priest forgives the one who confesses. Quite often in our times Confession takes place not in a booth but in a private office, sitting in chairs, in intimate conversation.

Jews are proud that there are no intermediaries in our religion, but I can tell you that as soon as new acquaintances of any religion discover that I am a rabbi they often spontaneously engage in confession. It can be very cathartic to have a religious person before whom to confess. The human need to confess one's wrongdoing and be forgiven and absolved of guilt is a powerful motivation.

In the Mass, the Liturgy of the Eucharist (Communion) follows after the Liturgy of the Word, which includes prayer, doctrinal statements and Scriptural readings. The consecrated wafers of unleavened bread and the consecrated wine are brought out. The worshipers line up and take turns approaching the altar. The priest places a piece of the matzah on the tongue of the worshiper or, more often in modern times, drops it into the upheld hands of the worshiper who places it on their own tongue. The priest gives the worshiper a sip of the wine and then wipes the lip of the cup. When the worshipers have received their wafer and wine they go back to their seats and take some moments in silent reflection as they allow the wafer to dissolve in the mouth, so that it is not treated as ordinary food. After the ceremony of Communion, the Mass comes to a conclusion.

Catholics and some other Christians believe in the doctrine of Transubstantiation. This means that during the sacred ceremony in the Mass the bread actually becomes the flesh of Christ and the wine actually becomes the blood of Christ, while simultaneously retaining its material nature as bread and wine. Thus, on the level of a religious mystery, the communicant actually partakes of the flesh and blood of Christ, who is divine. This is a matter of great discussion amongst Christians, and a Jew should not expect to comprehend it. As we shall see in a later chapter, Jews have been brought into this discussion in an unhappy way.

As we have already discussed, many Protestant denominations have diminished or done away with sacraments. Protestants are prone to interpret Communion as symbolic of the worshiper's personal relationship with Christ. While a Catholic has the opportunity for Communion on a daily basis, a Protestant church may offer communion only on Sundays, and often only once or twice a month rather than at every Sunday worship. The matzah and small cups of juice may be placed on trays and passed around, while the worshipers remain in their seats. When every worshiper who wishes has taken some, all will eat and drink together. There are even some contemporary churches which offer Communion to persons who have not been baptized. Regardless of such permission, it would not be right for a Jew to partake of Communion.

# CHAPTER TWENTY: THE LORD'S PRAYER

## Jesus' Personal Prayer

Here is the personal prayer of Jesus, which Christians call The Lord's Prayer, in King James Bible English:

Our Father who art in Heaven, hallowed be Thy name.

They kingdom come. They will be done on earth, as it is in heaven.

Give us this day our daily bread,

And forgive us our trespasses, as we forgive those who trespass against us,

And lead us not into temptation, but deliver us from evil.

Protestants add these words:

For thine is the kingdom and the power and the glory forever.

Christians recite this prayer in every worship service. It is found in two of the four Gospels, Matthew 6:9-13 and Luke 11:2-4 in a slightly shorter version.

An aside here on the textual history of the New Testament. The two Gospels of Matthew and Luke share a good amount of material which is not found in Mark. Text historians believe based on the evidence that Matthew and Luke shared two sources, the Book of Mark and a lost Gospel they call Q from the German Quelle, meaning "source." Jesus' prayer, then, would have come from the Q source and been copied by Matthew and Luke in slightly different forms.

## Personal Prayers of the Masters in Rabbinic Sources

In Judaism in the time of Jesus a person who wanted to become a rabbi became a disciple of a rabbi. Some rabbis established academies for rabbinic training. Others may have taken on promising young men as personal disciples. A disciple learned the Torah teachings that the master had internalized. More than that, the disciple attempted to live like the master, to absorb some of the divine spirit that was reflected in the Torah of the master. This attitude of internalizing the ways of the Master is well expressed in a Hasidic tale from a much later period. One disciple says to his friend who has just returned home, "What did you learn from the teachings of our Master?" The second disciple says, "I did not go to him to hear what he had to say, but to observe how he washes the dishes." Many modern-day Jews believe that the word "rabbi" means "teacher", but it actually means "master", referring to the relationship of the master to the disciples. The karate term "sensei" retains some of that flavor.

One expectation of disciples in ancient times is that the Master would teach them his personal prayer, which would exemplify the proper manner of prayer. The Talmud lists the personal prayers of a number of rabbinic masters. One of these prayers, the prayer of the 4$^{th}$ Century Babylonian sage Mar bar Ravina, is printed in every Jewish prayer book and is well known to every Jew who is familiar with Jewish worship. Here is a translation from the Hebrew:

O Lord, guard my tongue from evil and my lips from speaking deceit.

May my soul be humble and forgiving to all.

Open my heart, O Lord, to Your sacred Torah,

And may my soul eagerly seek to fulfill Your commandments.

Frustrate the designs of those who would do me ill and transform their thoughts.

Act for the sake of Your Name; act for the sake of Your power;

Act for the sake of Your holiness; act for the sake of Your Torah.

That Your loved ones may be delivered, O Lord,

Answer me and save me with Your redeeming power.

May the words of my mouth and the meditations of my heart

Be acceptable to You, O Lord, my Rock and my Redeemer.

Jesus' followers looked upon him as their Master and saw themselves as his disciples. Jesus was not a rabbi, but his disciples anxiously sought to pattern their own lives after his teachings and actions. It was only natural, then, that Jesus' followers would request of him a personal prayer.

Historical scholars question which words attributed to Jesus were actually spoken by him and which were attributed to him at a later time. There is near unanimous agreement that Jesus' personal prayer was spoken by him. The New Testament is written in Greek but Jesus spoke Aramaic. It is easy to translate the words of the Lord's Prayer into Aramaic and to see these words fitting into Jewish Aramaic thought patterns. That is one criterion in determining which words attributed to Jesus truly come from him.

**The Message of The Lord's Prayer**

Jesus' personal prayer is a typical expression of First Century Jewish piety. If we were to translate the words into modern idiom we would say: Heavenly Father, may people sanctify Your name. May You alone rule over the world. May people obey Your decrees as faithfully as do the stars in the sky (which follow the path You set for them.) Provide for our daily needs and forgive our wrongs as we deserve to the extent that we forgive the wrongs of others against our selves. Please do not put temptation in front of us so that we will not find it too difficult to do what is right and refrain from doing wrong.

To sanctify God's name means to praise God in prayer and speech and to live in such a way that one's deeds bring honor to the One who has commanded them. Jews of the First

Century fervently desired an end to the rule of the endless chain of empires (Assyria, Babylonia, Persia, Greece, Rome …) and for God to rule over the world directly. That is the coming of God's kingdom. We ask God to meet our needs, to forgive our sins, and to ease our path to a virtuous life.

It is notable that Jesus' personal prayer is devoid of Christian references. There is no reference to salvation through faith, no reference to a divine human Christ, no critique of the Judaism of the time that would call for a transformation to a new religion. Jews do not say the Lord's Prayer, nor should they. The act of speaking this prayer identifies a person as a disciple and follower of Jesus – that is, a Christian. In terms of content, though, the Lord's Prayer is a perfectly acceptable Jewish prayer.

Some historical scholars believe that the Lord's Prayer is a version of the Kaddish prayer, which is well known to Jews. The Kaddish opens with a request that God's name be sanctified in the world, followed by a request for God's kingdom – that is, for God to rule over the world directly. The Kaddish concludes with a prayer for God's peace to extend from heaven over all the earth and the Jewish people. The parallels to The Lord's Prayer are notable, although there are also notable differences. The Kaddish is the only Jewish prayer that is recited in Aramaic, not Hebrew. In antiquity the Kaddish was not part of the worship service; it was recited at the conclusion of a study session.

**The Lord**

The "Lord" in the title given to the Lord's Prayer is a reference to Jesus. The English word Lord is equivalent to the Hebrew word Adon. It refers to a noble or royal master, a person to whom a subject owes loyalty. It was typical in the pre-modern world for every person to have a lord. Peasants served the local nobleman who owned the land they worked. Knights served a nobleman or king who commanded their actions. The nobility held the king as their lord. God is the ultimate Lord of all humans, the highest ruler in the hierarchy of human society.

Jews use the word "our Lord", *Adonai*, to refer to the four-letter personal name of God. This name is the four letters yud-heh-vav-heh. The Name cannot be pronounced, and in its place Jews say Lord. Christians use the word Lord to refer to Jesus, often to distinguish Jesus the Son from God the Father as a person of the Christian Trinity. Jews and Christians might both use the word Lord in prayer, but they mean by it different things.

## The Lord's Prayer and the Twenty-Third Psalm

Jewish people who are not well acquainted with Jewish and Christian prayer often mistake the Twenty-Third Psalm for the Lord's Prayer. They may be surprised to learn that the Twenty-Third Psalm is actually a Jewish prayer, found in the Jewish Bible. They may have some familiarity with this popular Psalm because it is so often quoted. Not knowing the text of the Lord's Prayer but having heard of it, they may think this is it, because it begins with a reference to "the Lord." Since this confusion is so common amongst Jews, we will quote here the Twenty-Third Psalm in full, in the beloved King James English version:

The Lord is my shepherd, I shall not want.

He maketh me to lie down in green pastures. He leadeth me beside still waters.

He restoreth my soul.

He guideth me in straight paths (or, in the path of righteousness) for His name's sake.

Yea, though I walk through the Valley of the Shadow of Death

I shall fear no evil, for Thou art with me.

165

Thy rod and Thy staff, they comfort me.

Thou preparest a table before me in the presence of mine enemies.

Thou hast anointed my head with oil.

My cup runneth over.

Surely goodness and mercy shall follow me all the days of my life,

And I shall dwell in the house of the Lord forever.

This beautiful Psalm is recited by both Jews and Christians in times of anxiety and especially at funerals, with its promise of eternal life. It is not the Lord's Prayer. It is likely, though, that when Christians recite this Psalm it brings to mind Jesus as the shepherd leading his flock. This may be one reason that Jews confuse this Psalm with the Lord's Prayer. According to Jewish tradition, King David is the author of the Twenty-third Psalm. He drew on his boyhood experience as the shepherd of his father's flock.

# CHAPTER TWENTY-ONE: THE NICENE CREED

## The Nicene Creed

We believe in one God, The Father, the Almighty,

Maker of heaven and earth, Of all that is, seen and unseen.

We believe in one Lord, Jesus Christ, The only Son of God,

Eternally begotten of the Father. God from God, Light from Light,

True God from true God, Begotten, not made, Of one Being with the Father.

Through him all things were made. For us and for our salvation

He came down from heaven, By the power of the Holy Spirit

He became incarnate from the Virgin Mary, And was made a man.

For our sake he was crucified under Pontius Pilate.

He suffered death and was buried.

On the third day he rose again In accordance with the Scriptures.

He ascended into heaven And is seated at the right hand of the Father.

He will come again in glory to judge the living and the dead,

And his kingdom will have no end.

We believe in the Holy Spirit, the Lord, the giver of life,

Who proceeds from the Father and the Son.

With the Father and the Son he is worshiped and glorified.

He has spoken through the Prophets.

We believe in one holy catholic and apostolic Church.

We acknowledge one baptism for the forgiveness of sins.

We look for the resurrection of the dead, and the life of the world to come. Amen.

**Creeds in Christianity**

A creed is a statement of beliefs about God. The word comes from the Latin word credo which means, "I believe." Since Christians believe that salvation comes through faith, it is important to have correct faith, to believe in the right beliefs. Early in Christian history a number of creeds were developed to summarize the correct faith for a Christian. Some of these creeds are used in Christian worship. Amongst the most common are the Apostolic Creed and, most popular of all, the Nicene Creed. The Nicene Creed is accepted by virtually all Christians – Catholic, Orthodox and Protestant. The Nicene Creed is, one may say, the ultimate faith statement of a Christian.

The Nicene Creed was formulated at the Council of Nicea, an assembly of Christian bishops called together by the Roman Emperor Constantine I, the first Christian emperor, in the year 325. In the early centuries of Christianity, a variety of rival forms of Christianity had developed. Now that Christianity was to be the official religion of the Roman Empire, the Emperor saw it as desirable to have a single "correct" form of Christianity for all believers. Forms of Christianity which were not consistent with the correct version were suppressed by the power of the Empire. It is worth noting in relationship to the early Church councils the special status granted to Judaism. The Church could have declared Judaism to be a heresy of Christianity, a form of the Christian religion which denies the divinity of Christ. Had the Church done so (and there have been those who have argued for this view even in our own times) the Empire could have suppressed Judaism to the point that Jews and Judaism may have disappeared from the earth.

The Church chose instead to see Judaism as a separate religion and the Jews as the living members of God's Chosen People as spoken in the Hebrew Scriptures. Jews and Judaism were therefore granted protected, if inferior, status in the Christian world. We Jews should be thankful for this benefit. All forms of Christianity which did not conform to the official version expressed in the Nicene Creed were suppressed, and those Christians who did not change their beliefs to conform met an unhappy end.

Of the various forms of Christianity that had evolved by the 4th Century, some drew more from the wellsprings of Judaism and some drew less. The Christianity of the Nicene Creed is somewhere in the middle. It confirms that Christianity is a monotheistic religion and it confirms the Holy Scriptures which includes the Hebrew Bible. One can imagine other Christianities which could have emerged, some more like Judaism and some much less. The Christianity that became the standard, that of the Nicene Creed, retains a relationship with the Jewish roots of Christianity. Some Christians in the modern age see Christianity as a composite religion with a variety of Jewish and Hellenistic inputs. Some have called for Christians to increase the Jewish influence within Christianity, to develop a deeper relationship with Jews and Judaism as a way to strengthen their own Christianity. That call is possible because Christianity as it evolved never severed its connection to Judaism.

## Some Jewish Reactions to the Nicene Creed

Christians recite the Lord's Prayer and the Nicene Creed in their liturgical worship. To Christians these two texts seem part of a seamless whole, for they are one in the prayer life of a Christian. A Jew, by contrast, can see a great difference between the two. The Lord's Prayer seems familiar and accessible. It is much like Jewish prayer. The Nicene Creed

debated and crafted, and selected to the exclusion of other possibilities.

The Nicene Creed states that while there are three parts to the Trinity there is only one God, and all three are part and parcel of the one God. "Begotten not made" means that Jesus is an aspect of God's own being and not a creation by God. The Son becomes incarnate – that is, a flesh and blood human being – at a certain point in time, in the person of Jesus of Nazareth, but the Son as a person of the Trinity is eternally existent, for God does not come into being nor pass out of being. The Nicene Creed teaches that Jesus is both fully divine and fully human. It is a challenge to the imagination of a Christian to accept this paradox. It is understandable that many Christian individuals find it hard to accept the full implications of Jesus being a human being, while revering him as God, but this is what Christianity requires of the believer.

Since God is One, it is prohibited for a Christian to treat the three persons of the Trinity as separate deities. The oneness of God is expressed through each of the three persons. It is common in some branches of American Protestant religion to have an Angry Old Testament God of Judgment and a Gracious Jesus Christ of the New Testament. This view of the Angry Old Testament God has entered common parlance and is often referred to when natural disasters strike or when people act on their passion for vengeance. Jews naturally take offense at this characterization of the Old Testament God, since this is presumed to be the God that Jews worship. Those Christians who believe in the angry Old Testament God are only incidentally placing a judgment upon Judaism; the harsh Old Testament Father is, rather, part of their own belief system. As the Christian scholar Anthony Salderini once wrote, it is hard to get rid of this angry Old Testament God because many Christians love Him. The Christian issue for this view of God is that it is a dualistic view of Christianity which undermines the unity of the Trinity. One is not supposed to assign separate personalities or create a division of labor between the persons of the Trinity. The Jewish issue is our frustration that many Christians imagine that grace and forgiveness are unknown in Judaism. It is also a challenge for Judaism that many Jews, more familiar with popular culture than their own, have come to believe that the Angry Old Testament God is the God of their own religion.

For Jews, the ultimate expression of the absolute unity of God is our statement of faith from the Torah, (Deuteronomy 6:4) "Hear, O Israel, the Lord is our God, the Lord is One." Christians find a hint of the Trinity in this very verse. "The Lord, our God, the Lord" equals the Trinity. "Is One" equals the unity within the Trinity. Christians also find a hint of the Trinity in the three angels who visit Father Abraham to announce the coming birth of Isaac (Gen. 18). To Jews, the three angels are Michael, Gabriel and Raphael. What can we say? Christians use our Bible as their own holy book, and they read it in their own way. It is not a question of who is right and who is wrong. The "right" interpretation of these verses and many others has been an object of debate between Christians and Jews for millennia. Those with a modern historical understanding of the evolution of our Holy Scriptures and their later interpretation do not engage in such pointless arguments.

Jewish readers, you might expect me at this point to explain the Trinity. How can a Jew understand the Christians belief that God is Three and also One? If you would like this explained you are going to be disappointed. It is probably not possible for a Jew to understand the Trinity. It is difficult enough for a Christian. Amongst Christians there is an often-repeated saying of unknown origin: "The Trinity – try to understand it and you will lose your mind; try to deny it and you will lose your soul." One could fill a library with books that have been written by Christian scholars over the centuries explaining the meaning of the Trinity in Christian terms. That exploration will never cease as long as there are Christians. Since the Trinity is not within the Jewish belief system, we do not have to explain it. Be content to know that we accept our Christian neighbors as fellow monotheists.

The Kabbalah, the system of Jewish mystical thought, posits that God is expressed in the world through ten divine emanations, the Sefirot. When Christians began to study Kabbalah, some were indignant to discover that Jews believe in the Ten Sefirot. "Why is it," they asked, "that Jews refuse to believe in a three-in-one God, but they are willing to believe in a ten-in-one God?" There are significant differences between the Trinity and the Ten Sefirot, but it is still a challenging question. Not every question has an answer, especially when it comes to understanding God. Let us conclude this chapter in awe at the greatness of God and with humility over the limits of human understanding.

# CHAPTER TWENTY-TWO: EVANGELISM AND CONVERSION – WHO IS SAVED?

## Christian Mission

Christianity is a missionary religion. Christians feel an obligation to spread the word about Christianity and encourage conversions until the entire world is Christian. The Christian name for spreading the word about Christianity is "evangelism". Evangelism means "to spread the good news." It is similar in meaning to the word Gospel, the name for the four New Testament books which teach Christianity by telling the story of Jesus. An evangelist is any Christian who strives to convert others. A missionary is a person who has taken on evangelism as a profession for a period of time or as one's life's work. Most Jews in America have had the experience of being evangelized by a Christian friend or by a stranger who knocks on your door or accosts you on the sidewalk. We may have a persistent Christian friend who has taken on our conversion to Christianity as a personal project. Many Christians feel a special obligation to convert Jews to Christianity. There are professional missionary organizations that specifically target Jews.

Christian mission is founded on the belief that salvation is possible only through Christ. Christian souls will go to Heaven while non-Christian souls are condemned for eternity. It is therefore humane to bring every human being into the saving faith in Jesus as the Christ. To traditional Christians this means to encourage non-Christians to join the Church, to be baptized into God's true Church. Evangelical Protestant Christians focus more on the personal experience of being "born again" as a Christian. Evangelicals may even believe that no person raised as a Christian may call their self a Christian or be saved until they have had a personal conversion experience.

## Judaism and Mission

Judaism is not a missionary religion. One can identify at least three big reasons for this. The first reason is that Judaism is the religion of a single nation, the Jewish nation. Conversion to Judaism is a naturalization ceremony to enter the Jewish people. Nations in general are content to be who they are, distinct from other nations of the world. Most nations limit or restrict immigration. Jews are content for Jews to be Jewish. Most Jews do not feel any compulsion to bring non-Jews into the Jewish fold.

Another reason that Jews are not missionaries is that Jews do not believe that Judaism is the exclusive path to salvation. Just the opposite – Jews believe that it is harder for a Jew to achieve salvation. A Gentile can be saved by observing the Seven Laws that God gave to Noah – essentially, to be a good person. True beliefs are not required for a Gentile to be saved. A Jew, on the other hand, must observe 613 commandments from the Torah. The more educated in Torah a Jew becomes, the more demanding God becomes. It is the task of a Jew to jeopardize his or her own salvation by eliminating ignorance as an excuse. For example, Gentiles are not obligated to rest on the Sabbath day, but Jews are, and Jewish scholars are expected to exemplify proper Sabbath observance. Why should a Gentile risk God's judgment by becoming a Jew when that Gentile can more easily achieve personal salvation within their own religion? If a Gentile comes to a rabbi with a desire to convert the rabbi is obligated under Jewish law to attempt to discourage that Gentile by warning them of the difficulty of Jewish observance and reminding them of the diminished status of the Jewish people amongst the nations. Only a person who says "I know all of that and I desire to be a Jew anyway" is welcomed to begin Jewish studies.

176

A third reason that Judaism is not a missionary religion is that once the Roman Empire became Christian, conversion to Judaism was outlawed. The punishment in Christian lands for conversion to Judaism was to be burned alive at the stake. This punishment was meted out both to the convert and to the Jew who supervised the conversion. This situation put a damper on any Jewish missionary urge that may have existed. In the 18th Century a Polish count, Valentin Potocki, converted to Judaism and took the name Avraham ben Avraham. Especially because he was a nobleman, he was hunted down despite his best efforts to hide. He was captured and burned alive in 1749. It is only in very recent times and in modern countries that a person could safely convert to Judaism.

The idea of conversion to Judaism was controversial in the time of Jesus. The Sadducees believed that there is no such thing as conversion. Jewish identity is conferred by birth alone. The Pharisees actively sought out converts to Judaism. In Matthew 23:15 Jesus criticizes the Pharisees for seeking proselytes to Judaism. In the light of history this is surely an ironic passage. The author of Matthew was opposed to conversion. He represents Jesus as delivering his message only to the Household of Israel, only reluctantly accepting the reverence of Gentiles. At the end of the Book of Matthew a paragraph is appended which represents the ultimate Christian attitude to evangelism. The returned Christ speaks to the disciples and says to them, "All authority in heaven and earth has been given to me. Go therefore and make disciples of all nations, baptizing them in the name of the Father and of the Son and of the Holy Spirit, teaching them to observe all that I have commanded you." (Matthew 28:18-20)

In contemporary America the Reform Movement of Judaism has adopted the view that Judaism should compete in the open marketplace of religions that characterizes American society.

177

people. It was reported as a scandal that on his deathbed Disraeli recited the *Shema Yisrael* like a pious Jew.

Despite some famous cases of residual Jewish identity, the net effect of unreligious conversion was a great diminution in Jewish numbers. Many Jews who would not renounce Judaism to join another faith were happy to assimilate into a secular and not very religious society which was nominally Christian. Half the entire Jewish population of Germany disappeared in this manner. Descendants of converts from only one or two generations were counted as Jews by the Nazis, with the result that numerous believing Christians were murdered as Jews.

**Jews for Jesus and Messianic Jews**

The past few decades have seen the rise in America of a phenomenon never before seen in Christian history – Christians who evangelize to Jews by claiming not to be Christians at all, but to be Jews "completed" by faith in Christ. Historically, Christians would be outraged by such a posture. Engaging in Jewish practices was prohibited by the Church, and the first obligation of a Christian evangelist was to proclaim oneself to be a Christian.

The Jews for Jesus organization was created by a Baptist missionary who called himself Moishe Rosen. Rosen was frustrated that secular Jews who did not practice their own religion were nevertheless resistant to becoming Christian. He studied his subjects and came to the conclusion that their vestigial attachment to Jewish tradition was preventing their conversion. They dared not say to their parents "I am breaking the chain of Jewish tradition that goes back to our ancestors." Rosen's clever response was to allow his Jewish converts to keep their Jewish ethnic identity, while filling in their empty spiritual life with faith in Jesus. His converts would still be Jews, but now they would be Jews for Jesus. Rosen saw this as a transitional phase; his stated purpose was to move Jewish converts into mainstream Baptist churches as quickly as possible.

A different tactic was adopted by the Messianic Jews, a denomination sponsored by the Assemblies of God. The Messianics maintain their own churches which they call synagogues, and have their own pastors whom they call rabbis. They use Jewish ritual objects in their worship, assigning to these objects Christological meanings. There are now second and third generation Messianics. They perceive themselves as Jews but are not seen as such by practicing Jews.

Despite the devotion of Jews for Jesus and Messianics to the Jewish people and to the State of Israel, their theology is anti-Jewish. They see Judaism as an inadequate and incomplete religion which needs to be "completed" through faith in Jesus, whom they call Yeshua. The Christian beliefs of these groups are typical of the beliefs of Fundamentalist Protestant Christianity and are contradictory to the beliefs of Judaism.

In approaching the task of this book, I was concerned that some Jews might fear this work could be a subtle attempt to convert Jews by a Messianic missionary posing as a rabbi. I assure all readers that this is not the case. I hope that Jews who read this book will come away with a better understanding and a positive appreciation of Christianity. I hope that the knowledge gained will help Jews to be more faithful to the Jewish covenant with God. It is my belief that, while all are free in a free country to promote their religion to others, all true believers should begin by proudly announcing to others the name of the faith to which they subscribe. Deception, even for a holy cause, is contrary to God's purpose, for Truth is the Seal of God.

### Evangelism and Evangelical Christianity

American Jews must know that many Protestants consider themselves to be Evangelical Christians. This word sounds a lot like the word "evangelism", and it is closely related. Evangelism refers to the outreach of any Christian to bring non-Christians into Christianity. Evangelical refers to a specific form of Protestant Christianity. Evangelism is a big part of Evangelical Christianity. There are various denominations of Protestants who consider themselves to be Evangelical, and there are sub groups within some denominations who call themselves Evangelical. Evangelical Christians are characterized by certain traits:

Evangelicals put an emphasis on personal conversion, the experience of being "born again" as a Christian. People born into Christian families as well as non-Christians are encouraged to undergo conversion in this spirit.

Evangelicals put a great stress on faith. They see the saving grace of Jesus' death as an atonement for all sin as the central message of the Bible.

Evangelicals are Bible centered. They believe in deriving one's religion directly from reading the Bible, without the intermediacy of tradition or hierarchy.

Evangelicals are mission oriented, to spread the Word to all humankind.

Evangelical Protestants are often in conflict with Catholics. Some Evangelicals may not consider Catholics to be true Christians. Part of America's history is that there was a lot of anti-Catholic prejudice, especially in the 19th Century. Obedience to the Pope and to Church tradition and sacramentalism were openly derided. When John Kennedy was elected in 1960 as the first Catholic President of the United States, that was a big step for America. The years since that time have seen a big advance in mutual acceptance between Catholics and mainstream Protestants in America. They can visit each other's churches, and may accept as valid each other's baptisms. Despite this mutual acceptance, there are still

182

Evangelical Protestants in America who believe that Catholics need to convert to become Christians. Jews may be puzzled to hear such talk. It relates to the belief in the need for personal conversion as opposed to the Catholic view that those who are baptized in the Church are saved as Christians.

## Christian Acceptance of the Jewish Covenant with God

There are Christians, particularly conservative Evangelical Christians, who believe that God cannot hear the prayer of a Jew. Jews take offense at this position but it is not directed against us; it is a dramatic way of stating their own Christian belief that no one may approach the Father except through the Son, and there is no salvation except through faith in Jesus Christ.

There are many contemporary Christians who would like to validate Judaism, or Judaism and all other religions, while remaining true to their Christian faith. They may be moved by a desire to repent for a history of oppression against Jews and for the brutal conquests that paved the way for missionaries, or they may be moved by a desire to validate the redeemable humanity of all people, regardless of religion. They may have other motives. How can a Christian say that redemption is possible for followers of other religions while still holding that Jesus' death was necessary for the redemption of humankind?

One path is to say that God has made different covenants with different people. God's covenant with the Jews, the covenant of Torah and commandments, is valid for Jews alone, while God has provided the New Covenant, Christianity, to bring redemption to the Gentile nations.

Another path is to say that Christ is present in all religions, even if those religions do not acknowledge Christ. The problem with this liberal perspective is that it undermines another liberal value, which is to allow others to define themselves in their own terms.

Another path is to say that a Christian may have a Creation theology and a Salvation theology. The Creation theology may allow for the traditions and beliefs of other peoples, while the Salvation theology applies to Christian faith. Thus, missionaries may allow native peoples to keep their own traditions and rituals while bringing them to Christ.

This is just a sampling of ideas. Only a Christian can say what a Christian ought to believe. For a Jew it is sufficient to note that many contemporary Christians do believe that Judaism provides a valid path to God and salvation of the soul for Jews. In the words of the Prophet Samuel, "the Eternal One of Israel does not play false." (I Sam. 15:29) God's covenant with the Jewish people is valid for all time.

# CHAPTER TWENTY-THREE: FAITH VERSUS WORKS

In this chapter we explore the root difference between Christianity and Judaism, the contradiction that makes them two separate and distinct religions. We approach this topic with some trepidation because our intent is to simplify for the sake of clarity matters which are quite complex. We pray that God blesses this effort. Christians have been writing and debating for two thousand years about Faith versus Works. We will attempt to summarize their views in just a few pages.

### Paul Explains Faith in Jesus Christ in Contrast to Works

Paul, in his Epistles to the Christian communities of his time, explains for Christians the meaning of the doctrine of the Christ. Paul's words are the foundation for all Christianity. In order to explain the Christ, Paul asks himself a question which he then answers. His question is, "Why is the Christ necessary?" Why did God have to become human and die on the cross as a sacrifice of atonement for human sin? What was missing before this happened? Paul's answer, in large part, is that God's previous attempt to bring human beings to righteousness through the revelation of the Torah to the Jews ended in failure. The Gentiles remained unaware of God's law, and the Jews were unable to fulfill it. The Torah failed to justify humankind. It failed to make people righteous.

In Hebrew the word *tsaddik*, justified or righteous person, is often used to refer to a good person, but it has a more specific meaning. It means to be found innocent in a court case. This is the sense in which Paul uses the word. When humans stand before God's judgment they are found wanting and so condemned. Humans need something more to justify them before God. That something more, says Paul, is faith in Jesus as the Christ.

Paul lays out his thoughts on this matter most fully in his Epistle to the Romans. Paul contrasts Faith with Works. By Works Paul means what a Jew would call *mitzvot*. Mitzvot define the correct behaviors which justify a person before God. Where Paul, writing in Greek, uses the terms law and works, Jews should understand Paul to mean Torah and mitzvot.

Paul sees Torah and Christ as an either/or. If Torah is adequate for salvation of the human soul then Christ is extraneous and unnecessary. That is not an acceptable conclusion for Paul. Faith in Christ must then be a necessary prerequisite for the salvation of every soul, Jew or Gentile.

Paul sees value in the Torah even though he does not believe it brings salvation. Paul says: If not for the law I would not have known sin. (Romans 7:7) Paul sees this as both a positive and a negative. On the positive side, the law gives the Jew a definition of right and wrong, so that a Jew knows God's expectations. Paul contrasts this to the Gentiles, who have only their own moral conscience, which is often unreliable, to direct them. On the negative side, the gift of the law has not made people obedient to it. People know what is wrong and they do it anyway. Worse, because of some perversity in human nature, knowledge of God's prohibitions makes people more likely to transgress. Paul gives an example: because I know not to covet, I covet all the more.

Since people sin no matter what, even knowing God's law, the only thing that can save the human soul is an act of pure grace on God's part, an act of grace which leads to forgiveness of all human sins. This act of grace, says Paul, is Jesus' death on the cross. Access to this grace, says Paul, is available to all who believe. Jew and Gentile alike are saved through faith in Jesus Christ.

Surely, my Jewish friend, you are now thinking, "But does that mean that a Christian can sin at will, seeing that God's grace will save them anyway?" Paul has anticipated this question. He responds that the believer, having experienced God's saving grace through faith, will desire not to sin. To sin willfully after experiencing God's grace would be like a slave who has been set free yet continues to act as a slave. The saved person will demonstrate through works that they have been saved. Does this mean that the saved person will be completely without sin? If not, God's saving grace still functions, because faith is necessary and sufficient for salvation.

Paul is clear on the necessity of faith. He is less clear about the ongoing value of mitzvah, works. His words can be understood in different ways. This has led to differing interpretations by Christians. Catholics believe in faith and works as the path to salvation, while some branches of Protestantism insist on faith alone, with no role for works. This is a matter of great debate between Catholics and Protestants.

Paul attempts to demonstrate from the Torah itself that faith is superior to works. He relies on a verse about Father Abraham (Romans 4). God promises Abraham that his descendants will be numerous. The Torah says, "Abraham believed God, and it was reckoned to him as righteousness." (Gen. 15:6). Elsewhere in the Epistles, in Hebrews 11, there is a whole list of verses demonstrating that all the heroes of the Hebrew Bible were justified by faith. Jews read these verses differently. It says in Habbakuk 2:4, "The righteous shall live by their faith." Jews read this verse with an emphasis on "live", demonstrating the need to live by the mitzvot. Christians read this verse with an emphasis on "faith", demonstrating that only faith brings life. The same verse is used by Jews and Christians to uphold their contrasting views.

## Jewish Responses to Paul

What would Judaism be like today if Jews had not been forced by circumstance to constantly defend the concept of mitzvah against Christian challenges based on the teachings of Paul? Would Judaism have evolved on its own some different concept of the balance between faith and works? It is an intriguing question but there is no answer. The only Judaism that exists is a Judaism that was forced to respond to Paul's arguments from the First Century onward.

The earliest Jewish response to Paul is the elimination in Jewish worship of the recitation of the Ten Commandments. In its place, just before the Shema Yisrael, Jews recite a prayer thanking God for the loving gift of Torah, mitzvah and laws. Paul taught that the Ten Commandments are the only commandments that a Christian must observe. The very term "Ten Commandments" is a Christian term which reflects Paul's teaching. Jews would speak of these commandments as *Aseret Hadibrot*, the Ten Words. They differ from the other 603 commandments only in having been spoken directly by God to the people Israel, at Mount Sinai. In the Temple service the Ten Words were recited before the recitation of the Shema Yisrael. Presumably this practice continued in the early worship service after the destruction of the Temple. When Christian Jews began to stand up in assembly and shout "that is all!", the recitation was changed. The new prayer says (evening version): With everlasting love You have loved the House of Israel, teaching us Your Torah, its mitzvot, laws and judgments. ... We will rejoice forever in Your Torah and Your Mitzvot, for they are our life and our length of days, and on them we will meditate day and night. May Your love never depart from us...

This prayer responds directly to Paul's arguments. God's grace is represented precisely by the giving of the Torah. The Torah is a sign of God's love, and not of God's wrath. By learning and living the law, Jews attain life.

188

*Pirkei Avot*, the Saying of the Sages, is the favorite and best-known section of the Talmud for Jews. It has been called "the Jewish Sermon on the Mount" because it contains pithy aphorisms for right living. The six chapters of the *Pirkei Avot* each conclude with the following passage: Rabbi Hananyah ben Akashia said, "The Blessed Holy One was pleased to make Israel worthy; therefore God gave them a copious Torah and many commandments, as it is said, 'It pleased the Lord, for His righteousness' sake (can be translated as: to justify His righteous ones), to magnify the Torah and make it honorable.'" This passage, which is not original to *Pirkei Avot* and was originally found in Tractate *Makkot*, is brought six times as a Jewish response to Paul. The commandments are multiplied, not to give humans opportunity to stumble, but to give humans opportunity to achieve merit with God. God does not so much gaze upon our failures, our sins, as God acknowledges the many times we have striven to fulfill God's will. Every mitzvh is an opportunity for justification, and there is a mitzvah for every occasion.

These arguments are not brought to argue with Christians, but to convince Jews to remain faithful to Judaism in the face of conversionary efforts.

Jews do not have our own version of the debate between faith and works. Faith played a minimal role in traditional Judaism. If a Jew lived to the best of their ability according to the commandments, no one ever asked them what they believe. The Jewish teaching on faith is that "the Commander is inherent in the commandment." We know that God is loving because we are commanded to love, and we love. We know that God cares for the sick because we are commanded to heal the sick, and we provide medical care. And so forth.

Judaism does have an internal debate on study versus works. Is it more important to learn Torah or to live by the Torah? A

189

this Jewish understanding. Based on this verse, Jews believe that humans may overcome the tendency to sin using their own inner resources, though it is difficult.

**Modern Views on Human Nature**

The Enlightenment generated a fresh study of human nature, independent of Christianity and Judaism. Some modern philosophers, like John Locke, determined that humans are evil by nature. The American Constitution's checks and balances, influenced by Locke, are intended to counter humankind's corrupting tendencies. Other modern philosophers, such as Jean-Jacques Rousseau, held that human beings are innocent by nature. It is only bad culture and bad education which lead to evil. The Enlightenment view that human beings are good by nature is, essentially, Christianity turned upside down. It may be seen as a secular revolt against Christianity. Many modern-day people who hold to Rousseau's view take a relative view towards morality, that sin as such does not exist. It is no longer popular to denounce sin, even from the Christian or Jewish pulpit. One of the most powerful counter-arguments to the claim that people are naturally good, the novel *Lord of the Flies*, was written in 1954 by British author William Golding, a Christian though not a member of any church.

The father of modern psychiatry, Sigmund Freud, discovered the unconscious human mind. He taught that the expressed human self, the ego, derived from unacknowledged internal conflicts between the id, or basic drive, and the superego, or conscience. Freud described the mechanisms through with the human mind works out inner conflicts. Unsuccessful conflict resolution leads to neurosis and worse. It has long been noted that Freud's psychology closely parallels the rabbinic view of the human personality as deriving from the inner conflict between the good impulse and the evil impulse. Freud never had any Jewish education, so there can be no direct relationship

192

between his view and that of the Sages. One could imagine that there is a Jewish way of looking at the world which Freud inherited from his Viennese Jewish environment, and this influenced his scientific thinking. It is possible. Modern psychology has moved away from Freud in many respects, though it retains Freud's basic insight that the unconscious mind is responsible for many of our actions.

Some modern psychologists have suggested that human free will is an illusion and our actions are entirely the result of hard-wired biological impulses and external stimuli. If that extreme view were the case, then Christianity and Judaism would both be rendered moot. More recent studies have demonstrated that even our genetically determined behaviors do not necessarily express themselves, depending on many factors. Our actions derive from a mixture of genetic heritage, environmental factors, educational inputs, culture, and personal decision making. Both Christianity and Judaism depend upon the ability of human beings to make our own decisions at least within a limited but highly significant realm. We cannot choose the race or economic class or nationality into which we are born, but we can choose for or against God. Christianity and Judaism agree that human beings are capable of a lot of evil, but also great good. Rabbi Akiva said: Everything is in the hands of Heaven except for the fear of Heaven (by which he means, our moral decision making).

Christology, and a new interest in the actual person of Jesus. This new movement led to the famous Search for the Historical Jesus, a search which still continues, now in its third or fourth phase. Hard as it is for people of today to imagine, before the 19th Century no one attempted to write a biography of Jesus. The Christian focus was on Jesus' salvational role as the Christ. The modern attempt to write the biography of Jesus forced scholars to confront the contradictions between the four Gospels. It also brought them to a need to understand Judaism at the time of Jesus, without which one could never understand Jesus the man. A new appreciation of the connection between Judaism and Christianity has resulted from this line of study. That is good news, but in the early stages of the Search for the Historical Jesus not all the news was good. The Search began at the very same time that anti-Semitism was building in Europe, leading towards the Holocaust. That, and the unfortunate tendency to view Christianity and Judaism as opposites, led Christian historical scholars to some negative views of the Judaism of the First Century as well as of contemporary Judaism.

Divine grace is expressed in human relationships as love. Love in ancient times was not thought of as an emotion but as an action, treating others as one ought to treat a close relative. The new Christian emphasis on religion as ethics caused post-Enlightenment Christians to focus on Jesus' teachings of love. Jesus taught, "Love your enemies." Jesus taught the Golden Rule: "Do unto others as you would have others do unto you." Three times in the Gospel of Matthew, Jesus repeats the words of Leviticus 19:18, "You shall love your neighbor as yourself." In one presentation Jesus is shown to be quoting Jewish Scriptures, but in another he seems to come up with the aphorism on his own, and in the third he is contrasting "Love your neighbor" to "Hate your enemies." This contrast has caused some people to believe that Judaism actually teaches hatred towards enemies. There is no such teaching in the Jewish Bible or elsewhere in Judaism. Jesus might have been speaking of all-too-normal human behavior. Or, he may have been thinking of the teaching of the Essenes, the Dead Sea Scrolls group, who indeed teach to love one's fellow disciples and to hate outsiders. Hate here, like love, does not mean a feeling. It means to limit interpersonal and commercial relationships with those who are not members of the group. Regardless, it is clear enough to Jews that Jesus was relying on traditional Jewish sources when he said to love your neighbor as yourself. In Jewish tradition, the founding Sages Hillel and Rabbi Akiva also refer to "love your neighbor" as the essence of the Scriptures.

The anti-Semitic way of representing Jesus' teaching of love is that Judaism teaches harsh judgment and hatred, unrelieved by any notion of grace or forgiveness. This mis-representation of Judaism was often based on the twice-repeated Torah passage "eye for an eye and tooth for a tooth." In both biblical law and later Judaism, "eye for an eye" means equality before the law. It means that every human eye and tooth is of the same value, regardless of the social status of the perpetrator and the victim. "Eye for an eye" in the anti-Jewish reading has been interpreted as a demand for vengeance. Mahatma Ghandi, tragically, understood the phrase this way when he famously stated "an eye for an eye makes the whole world blind." Ghandi was surely right that vengeance taking is destructive and never-ending, but it is unfortunate that his teaching ended up being based on a Scriptural interpretation that is harsh towards Judaism.

The New Testament God of grace has too often been contrasted in Christian preaching to an Old Testament God of judgment and vengeance.

197

Hades. The "shades" of people that outlast death to sleep in Sheol are something less that what we would call a "soul." The Sdducees held to this ancient belief. Sadducees are disdained in both the New Testament and rabbinic literature for not believing in life after death.

The Greek philosopher Plato developed a concept of the afterlife of the soul. (see *The Republic*.) Plato taught that the human person consists of two parts, body and soul. At death the body returns to the earth, while the souls of the righteous go to eternal reward in a heavenly afterlife. Jews became aware of this concept of the afterlife of the soul after the conquests of Alexander the Great, when the Greek Empire brought Greek philosophy and culture to the Middle East. The mixture of Greek and Ancient Near Eastern cultures led to a new hybrid culture called Hellenism. The doctrine of body and soul, so well known in modern culture that we take it for granted that all human beings are such a composite, was spread through Hellenistic culture.

We first hear of the uniquely Jewish doctrine of resurrection in the literature that followed the successful revolt of the Maccabees against the Syrian Greek Empire (135-132 BCE). Considering the close association of the doctrine of resurrection with the Pharisees, it seems likely that the parties of the Pharisees and Sadducees arose during the Maccabee rebellion. The doctrine of resurrection is promoted especially in the Second Book of Maccabees. First Maccabees is a political history of the rebellion, written to support the leadership claims of the Hasmonean rulers. Second Maccabees was composed to extol the martyrs of the rebellion and to teach the new doctrines that arose in response to King Antiochus' suppression of Judaism and the Jewish reaction. In Second Maccabees Chapter 8, a woman and her seven sons are arrested by King Antiochus. The sons go to their death one by one rather than submit to the king's demand that they worship an idol and eat pork. The sons, in their final speeches, teach the doctrine of resurrection and answer objections. Those who are maimed, for example, will be reborn whole with all their limbs. The mother declares that the miracle of resurrection is no greater than the miracle of birth by which her sons came into life.

As we reconstruct the history of the idea of resurrection, it would seem that the Pharisees accepted the Greek concept of life after death but rejected the Greek concept of body and soul. The Pharisees created their own doctrine of the afterlife in which people exist as a whole, die as a whole, and are reborn as a whole. To reiterate, because this is difficult for modern people to grasp, in the doctrine of resurrection there is no soul that departs the body at death to be rejoined with the body at the resurrection.

In the time of Jesus, the doctrines of resurrection and of the eternal soul were separate and distinct. The Gospels contain a number of stories of Jesus' reappearance to certain disciples in the days after his crucifixion. In some of these stories Jesus appears as a resurrected person, while in other stories he appears in spirit. We can reconstruct that these stories originated with separate groups of believers who held to difference concepts of the afterlife.

What confuses the matter for us is that both Jews and Christians ultimately accepted both doctrines of the afterlife, even though they are in many ways contradictory. Logically, if there is a heavenly afterlife for the soul, what need is there of resurrection, and vice versa? Scholars may have thought about this contradiction, but most believers were untroubled. In Jewish prayer, for example, there is a pair of prayers for the body and for the soul in the morning blessings, while there is a prayer for resurrection in the second blessing of the Amidah prayers. In general, those of a more rational and philosophical bent have shown a preference for the doctrine of the eternal soul, while traditional believers prefer the doctrine of resurrection.

The Gospels present a mixed evaluation of the Pharisees. In part this derives from historical memories of Jesus' interactions with Pharisees in Jerusalem, which seem to have been generally positive, but the stories are driven by later conflicts between early Christians and Pharisaic rabbinic leaders of the Jews. Most stories of Jesus and the Pharisees have a positive inner core with a negative introduction and conclusion which were probably added later. On the one hand the Pharisees, after they consolidated their control of Jewish leadership, attempted to suppress Christianity as a prohibited heresy. That made Christian leaders after the year 70CE anti-Pharisee. On the other hand, the Pharisees upheld the doctrine of resurrection which was required in Christianity to explain Jesus' rise from the dead after his crucifixion. Christians needed to support the Pharisees in order to support the doctrine of resurrection. That is a source of pro-Pharisee feeling for early Christians.

**Resurrection in later Judaism and Christianity**

The doctrine of resurrection became an established belief in both religions. The Pharisees and their successors, the Rabbis, were hard pressed to find Scriptural support for this belief. The rabbis responded defensively by claiming that, if they had to, they could derive the doctrine of resurrection from every single verse in the Bible. They also declared that the rejection of belief in resurrection is one of the signs of the Epicurean heretic who will have no place in the World to Come. The divine origins of the Torah, the supremacy of Moses as a prophet, and the doctrine of resurrection were designated as obligatory Jewish beliefs.

Paul had a novel view of the general resurrection which he describes in detail in his First Epistle to the Corinthians,

Chapter 15. Paul believed that at the resurrection people would receive spirit bodies rather than physical bodies. Those who are resurrected to life would be free from lower bodily functions and could spend their time in higher pursuits such as the contemplation of God.

The Talmudic Sages taught that there is a treasure chest of special dew under the throne of God in the highest heaven. When the time comes for the Resurrection, God will send this dew upon the earth, and it will raise up the dead. The Sages also speculated that there is a tiny bone at the base of the human spine which is indestructible, and which will be the foundation for each new human body to be constructed.

The Medieval Jewish philosopher Saadia was troubled by the logical problem of which person would receive which atoms to reconstruct their body, if an atom were shared by two individuals at separate times. Saadia proposed that by divine fiat no atom that had ever been part of any human body was ever again used for any other human body. All such atoms are reserved for the Resurrection. We now know that the human body is constantly shedding material and generating new material, which complicates the question of the material source of resurrected bodies.

The Jewish philosopher Maimonides created a sensation in the 12th Century when he rejected the doctrine of resurrection. Maimonides was forced by public opinion to publish a defense of resurrection. This essay, if taken at face value, defends the doctrine, but if one reads between the lines Maimonides appears to be mocking the belief. After Maimonides' death, when his works spread from Arab lands and reached the more pious Christian realms of Europe, a great controversy broke out in France between Jewish supporters and opponents of Maimonides, primarily concerning the doctrine of resurrection. The anti-Maimonideans went to the King of France, Louis IX, who was burning Christian heretics, and asked him to burn Maimonides' books. The King of France gladly obliged, and afterwards decided to burn all Jewish books. After some twenty wagon loads of Talmud volumes were burned, the Jews were forced to band together and drop their battle. The conflict over the doctrine of resurrection was never resolved.

In the modern era, resurrection comes under attack as being contrary to science and reason. The believers in resurrection in the First Century believed that the universe was only a few thousand years old. Those who hoped for resurrection believed that it would happen soon and that they would return to a world just like the one they departed upon their mortal death. Now that we know that the universe is about fifteen billion years old, and with all the changes that have taken place in society and in technology since antiquity, what place is there for resurrected human beings in the world? Would people from the time of Jesus be pleased to be reborn into the 21st Century, or would they feel lost and lonely? Despite these challenges, there are religious scholars in both Christianity and Judaism who uphold the traditional doctrine. Most persons in our time do not take resurrection literally even if they use the word in traditional contexts like prayer.

When I taught college students, I observed that when my Christian students spoke of the resurrected Christ they actually conceived of his return in the spirit. They did not understand resurrection as a return to bodily life. This made me curious so I asked some priests, who all perfectly understood the doctrine of resurrection and its distinction from the doctrine of the spiritual afterlife. I got the impression that the general public is not as aware of the meaning of resurrection as the educated priesthood.

The Reform Movement of Judaism in 19th Century Europe and America actively rejected the doctrine of resurrection as being inconsistent with modern science. Orthodox Jews challenged the Reformers on matters like head covering in worship and use of instrumental music in Sabbath worship, but they never publicly challenged the reformers on resurrection. It has not been an issue in Christian-Jewish relations that most modern-day Jews do not believe in resurrection. It would seem that the doctrine lacks passionate public defenders in our times. For the most part, modern people think in terms of body and soul as distinct aspects of human being. Scientific and atheistic attacks on the doctrine of the soul get far more religious pushback than attacks on the doctrine of resurrection.

# CHAPTER TWENTY-SIX: AFTERLIFE, HEAVEN AND HELL

The popular view of Heaven and Hell is well known from Hollywood movies, New Yorker Magazine cartoons, and other media. Good souls enter the pearly gates of heaven. There they receive a white robe, a harp and a set of angel wings. They stand around on puffy white clouds. God presides in Heaven, which sits above the earth.

Below the earth lies Hell. The wicked are condemned to spend eternity in Hell, a place of punishment. Hot fires burn the condemned souls. Satan, the Devil, presides over Hell. The Devil is assisted by his cohort of fallen angels, the demons. They pass their time tormenting the souls of the damned. The Devil has red skin, with goat horns on his head and a pointed tail behind. The Devil is the enemy of both God and humankind.

This view of Heaven and Hell, with some variations, is common to Christianity and Islam. Muslims imagine Heaven as a garden of delights, with delectable food and drink and other pleasures.

Many American Jews hold the mistaken opinion that Jews do not believe in the afterlife, and Heaven and Hell are purely Christian notions. That is not true. The World-to-Come is mentioned over three thousand times in rabbinic literature. For millennia Jews strove to live a good life, and even went to their death as martyrs, with the hope of achieving eternity in the next world. It is hard to know how this misconception became so widespread. Possibly it is because Jewish education in America is minimal for most Jews, and teachings about life after death somehow did not find a place in the abbreviated curriculum. The Jewish religion always placed more emphasis on life in this world, with the thought that the next life will then take care of itself. "Rabbi Jacob said: This world is the antechamber to the world-to-come. Prepare yourself in the ante-chamber so that you may make an entrance to the banquet hall." (Pirke Avot 4:21)

## Evolution of the Concept of Heaven and Hell

Christianity has a more elaborate and vivid concept of Heaven and Hell than does Judaism. Some of this may be due to theological emphasis. Much is due to great works of literary imagination by Christian authors such as John Milton and Dante as well as Christian painters who portrayed scenes from the afterlife. The Fourteenth Century Italian poet Dante Alighieri, commonly referred to as Dante, wrote a great poem in three parts, *The Divine Comedy*. The three parts describe Paradise (Heaven), Purgatory, and the Inferno (Hell.) Dante's Inferno is the most popular of the trilogy. In the poem, the writer takes a tour of the three regions of the afterlife. Hell is divided into multiple regions, each dedicated to the punishment of a particular type of sin. John Milton wrote *Paradise Lost*, published in 1667, an epic poem which focuses on Satan's fall from Heaven into Hell. These great poets generated a depiction of the afterlife upon which modern media images are largely based.

The concept of a heavenly reward for good souls originates in the philosophy of Plato, as we have mentioned in the previous chapter. Plato taught that a person has a mortal body and an immortal soul, which goes on to heavenly reward if a person lives a just and pious life. The concept of Hell as a place of fiery eternal punishment originates with certain Jewish sects from around the time of Jesus. Although Hell originates in Jewish thought, the concept of Hell has not found much of a place in Judaism. The early rabbis did not like the idea of Hell because it is associated with Gnostic, dualistic notions that offended their monotheism. The standard Jewish teaching is that whatever reward awaits the righteous in the afterlife, that reward is denied to the wicked. The wicked simply die forever. Nevertheless, Hell continues to hold a place in Jewish folk religion. Heaven was called Gan Eden, the Garden of Eden, as it is called also in Islam. Hell is called Gehinnom, the Valley of Hinnom. This is the location where, according to the Book of Kings, idol worshiping Israelites threw their babies into a fire to worship the Canaanite god Moloch. (In real life the babies were "baptized" by being passed over a fire.) A Jewish legend has Isaac sitting at the gates of Hell, preventing any man who is circumcised from entering there. Jews say the Kaddish prayer to speed the soul of their loved ones through the year of purgation in Gehinnom so that they may go more quickly to their eternal reward in Heaven. In Christian thought this purgation of souls takes place in a separate location, neither Heaven nor Hell, called Purgatory. The souls of persons who are mostly righteous must be punished in Purgatory for their earthly sins before they may enter Paradise, while the souls of the wicked go directly to Hell.

Jewish Heaven does not have harps and wings. There are various ideas about Heaven, with no requirement to believe one or another. Some Talmudic rabbis thought of Heaven as a place where the righteous sit on thrones, basking in the glow of God's light. That is similar to Christian notions. The most usual Jewish idea of Heaven is that it is the Yeshiva (Torah Academy) on High, where the righteous sit at a long table like the table in the Jewish schoolhouse and discuss words of Scriptural interpretation for eternity. Metatron, chief of the angels, sits at the head of the table as Dean of the Yeshiva on High. Those persons who did not attend gladiator games in life will get to see the final staged battle between Leviathan and the Bull of Heaven, after which the bodies of both great creatures will be roasted for the Feast of the Righteous. While Christians get a harp and wings, Jews get a seat at the study table.

210

Christians and Jews share the idea that basking in God's light is a pleasure that never diminishes for eternity.

Many Americans believe that when good souls go to Heaven, they become angels. This is not a correct understanding of religious tradition. Angels are immortal beings without physical bodies created by God at the time of Creation. Heaven is their eternal home. The souls of the righteous become immortal and go to Heaven, but they do not become angels. It is never clear whether this is the same Heaven as that inhabited by angels, or a different heavenly location. When it comes to the Afterlife, the religious imagination has free reign.

## Satan, or the Devil

People who believe there is a Devil call him Satan, but in Jewish belief Satan is not the Devil. The angel Satan makes his appearance in some of the final books of the Bible, books that were written during the Persian period. As we discussed in our chapter on Dualism, the idea of Satan was influenced by dualistic Persian religion. Satan in the Hebrew Bible is a resident of Heaven and a loyal servant of God. Satan is the prosecuting attorney in God's court. The word *satan* is an old Hebrew term for "prosecuting attorney." The biblical Satan is the enemy of humankind, because he wants God to convict us for our sins, but Satan is not the enemy of God.

A belief arose in some Late Second Temple Jewish circles that at the time of the Creation some of the angels rose in rebellion. With Satan as their leader, these angels attempted to take over the cosmos. God made war on the rebellious angels, defeated them, and cast them down into a pit of eternal fire, Hell. Satan became the Devil. Satan and his demon angels took vengeance on God by seducing Adam and Eve into disobedience, leading to their moral downfall and their expulsion from the Garden of Eden. Since that time, the Devil and God have been struggling for control of human souls, individually and collectively. From

211

this belief come the many stories about people selling their soul to the Devil in exchange for earthly glory, from Doctor Faustus to the blues guitarist Robert Johnson.

Belief in the Devil was well known amongst First Century Jews. In Matthew 4 and in Luke 4 Satan tempts Jesus, attempting to lure him from his mission with various offers. Is this Satan character the heavenly Prosecutor of the Hebrew Scriptures, or the Devil who is the enemy of God? From the context it could be either one. We see in the Book of Job that Satan may receive permission from God to attempt to lure human beings into evil ways. The same theme arises in some rabbinic legends. Or, this story may reflect a belief that the Devil is attempting to thwart God's purpose by tempting Jesus.

Ultimately, rabbinic Judaism rejected the belief in the Devil because of its dualistic theology. The Rabbis repeatedly affirmed that there is nothing in the universe that is not under the rule of God, except for the moral choices of human beings. Belief in the Devil as a counter force and enemy to God, with its origins in ancient Judaism, became significant to the belief systems of Christianity and Islam. In Milton's *Paradise Lost*, the Devil is the central character, as an eternally rebellious and defiant being who would rather suffer for eternity than submit to the rule of God. God is the hero of the story, but the Devil gets most of the good lines.

The Devil is called by other significant names. Lucifer, "the light giver", is a name for the planet Venus. Ancient Israelites, like other ancient peoples, associated the heavenly bodies with forces of nature, what we would call the mathematical laws of nature, and also with angels as we picture them, winged human-like immortal creatures with names that define their tasks, like Gabriel and Rafael. Angels, natural laws, and stars are one and the same. Each angel was created with one task which it fulfills faithfully, like a natural law. The stars in the

212

sky, marching in predictable lockstep across the sky, are angels that do God's bidding, and were seen by many as one and the same as the angels. The chief angel is the brightest star in the sky, the planet Venus. As in human politics, it is most often the second-in-command who rebels. The Devil is originally Lucifer, the brightest and most beautiful of the angels. Falling stars, which we know as meteorites, may have suggested to the ancients that there were disobedient angels who lost their place in the heavenly expanse.

The Devil is also called Beelzebub, a form of the Hebrew name *Baal Zevuv*, "Lord of the Flies." This was a name Israelites used to mock the Canaanite god Baal, who was given various appellations including *Baal Tzafon*, "Baal of the North" and *Baal Zevul*, "Baal of the Palace". Through this name the Devil becomes associated with pagan deities, suggesting that the Canaanites were Devil worshipers.

We have noted before that the Kabbalah often adopts religious positions that were common in Medieval Spanish Catholicism. The Zohar represents the snake in the Garden of Eden as a Devil-like creature, and the Zohar speaks often of demonic forces. The demonic forces in the Kabbalah do not have independent power. They derive their power by mirroring God's goodness. This may be an attempt to make the belief in demonic forces "safe" for monotheism. Kabbalah is undeniably more dualistic than Rabbinic Judaism. The prevalence of the demonic in Kabbalah may also be because Kabbalah brings much of the popular folk tradition back into mainstream Judaism. The Devil was always present in Jewish folklore.

## Conclusions

In general, we may say that the Devil does not have a place in Judaism. There is no Hell in Judaism, either as a place of punishment for the wicked nor as a home for rebellious demon angels. Hell, and the Devil, do appear in Jewish folklore, as they never completely disappeared from the Jewish consciousness. Hell, and the Devil, play a much larger role in Christianity and in Islam. The story of the Devil arose in ancient Judaism but found its home elsewhere. This may account for why Jews find it difficult to comprehend what Jews believe in these matters and how our religion differs from that of the other monotheistic faiths.

When Christians tell a story or joke about the newly departed being judged by St. Peter at the gates of Heaven, a Jew could faithfully tell the same joke, substituting the Archangel Gabriel for St. Peter. Jews and Christians have parallel beliefs about being judged at the Pearly Gates and then being granted entry into Heaven.

Jews should know that Judaism does confirm an afterlife, with reward for goodness, but the nature of that reward is open to discussion. The rabbinic Sages said that the rewards of the afterlife, or of resurrected life on earth, are temporary. After a long time, God will institute the World to Come, which is completely indescribable, but which is the sure inheritance of the righteous. Historic Christianity placed a much greater emphasis on holding out the rewards of Paradise and the punishments of Hell as motivation for faith and right living in this world.

# CHAPTER TWENTY-SEVEN: APOCALYPTIC CHRISTIANITY AND JUDAISM – AWAITING THE END OF TIME

We have noted that it is usually a mistake to represent Judaism and Christianity as exact opposites, even though this is too often done. When it comes to such central concepts as faith and works, salvation of the soul, grace and judgment, afterlife, monotheism and dualism, and more, Christianity and Judaism present differently nuanced responses to similar questions. Sometimes the two religions diverge greatly in their responses to the great questions, and sometimes their responses are similar. There is a great deal of convergence when we compare apocalyptic beliefs in Judaism and Christianity, concerning those who believe that the end of time is imminent. In America we associate the end-time scenario with conservative Fundamentalist Christians. Similar beliefs are found amongst some West Bank Israeli settlers, who saw Israel's 1967 victory in the Six Day War as a sign of the approaching end of time. Apocalyptic movements have arisen with regularity in both Christianity and Judaism, following a similar script.

## Apocalypse and Prophecy

The era of classical prophecy ended shortly after the return of the Jews from Babylonian exile in about 500 BCE. Haggai, Zacharia and Malachi are the final biblical prophets. With some overlap, prophecy was succeeded by a new type of religious message known as apocalypse.

The Greek word apocalypse means "a peek behind the curtain." The curtain in question is that which separates Heaven from Earth. The apocalyptic preacher sees behind the curtain where God's plan for the human future is made known. Typically, in apocalyptic preaching, what is revealed is that "the end is near." Because of this trait, the term "apocalypse" is synonymous with a belief in the imminent end-time.

215

Apocalypse differs from prophecy in a number of respects. The classical prophet confidently states "Thus says the Lord….". The apocalyptic preacher dares not presume such intimacy with God. Typically, in apocalypse, the writer is taken on a journey to the heavenly world by an angel messenger. God's will is revealed through the messenger rather than by direct divine speech. The messenger shows the writer puzzling images and visions and then explains them as predictions of events about to occur. Part of the attraction of the apocalyptic literary style is that the angel reveals heavenly secrets to the chosen recipient as if in private conversation. The reader gets the feeling of being privy to divine secrets that are hidden from the rest of humankind.

Prophecy placed a premium on human moral responsibility. The prophets spoke not so much about what will happen, as what might happen if the Israelites do not become more obedient to God's demand for social justice. In apocalyptic writing there is virtually no element of human choice in determining the future. The times and eras of history are all predetermined. People can only choose, if they get to choose at all, to be on the right side as events unfold according to God's predetermined plan.

The biblical prophets warned against disaster if the people did not shape up. After the disasters of the Assyrian and Babylonian exiles actually happened, the prophets spoke words of consolation and future hope. Apocalyptic thought invites and welcomes conflict, war and catastrophe. Things have to get worse before they can get better. The very worst must precede the very best, the triumph of God's justice on earth. Catastrophes are the birth-pangs of the final redemption. Ancient apocalyptic thinkers invited war between the world's empires. Modern apocalyptic believers think in terms of nuclear war, environmental disaster, and world-wide cultural clashes.

Apocalyptic writers typically express their vision of the future in elaborate imagery and metaphors. "The moon will drip blood and the sun will shine at midnight", and the like. It is interesting to note that while apocalyptic writers and, later in time, mystical writers claim to have inherited the mantle of prophecy, their literary tone distinguishes them as a different phenomenon. Only prophets have ever managed to sound like prophets. Apocalypse has its own style which is instantly recognizable.

Recent times have seen apocalyptic writing enter the secular realm. *The Celestine Prophecy* is a New-Age apocalypse that was at the top of the best-seller list for many years. *Ishmael: A Novel* is an environmentalist apocalypse in which a talking gorilla takes the role of the angel-messenger.

**The Rise of Apocalyptic Beliefs in Second Temple Judaism**

Apocalypse is based on certain passages in the Hebrew Bible. The prophet Ezekiel was a classical prophet and not an apocalyptic writer, but his vision of the future downfall of the Babylonian Empire has influenced apocalyptic thinking. Ezekiel observed the Babylonian conquest of Judah and the exile of the Judeans. In Ezekiel Ch. 38 and 39 he predicts the downfall of Babylon in a great war. In order to escape the interest of the Babylonian censors, Ezekiel uses code words. Gog is the Emperor, and Magog is his country. This coded language is sufficiently vague that later generations of apocalyptic readers apply it to their own enemy. In our times Magog has been identified as the Soviet Union, and more recently as Saddam Hussein's Iraq or as Islamic jihadists.

The Book of Daniel is the last book of the Hebrew Bible to be written. It contains numerous apocalyptic elements. Of particular influence is Daniel Ch.7, in which the rise and fall of empires is visualized as the appearance before God of various beasts, each more ferocious than the last. There is in this vision something of the predetermination of history that is typical of apocalyptic. At the end of the chain appears a human-like figure who is granted an everlasting kingdom that will not fall. This is most likely originally intended as a prediction of the ultimate triumph of the Kingdom of Judah over all the empires. It is understood by Christians to speak of the eternal reign of Christ.

The prophet Zachariah has an angel messenger to show him God's plan. In Zachariah Chapter 4, the prophet is shown unusual images which the angel explains represent the glorious return of the High Priest Joshua and the Judean King Zerubbabel to leadership of the Kingdom of Judah within the Persian Empire. Zerubbabel apparently did not listen to Zechariah's advice to rule by divine spirit and not seek power, because shortly afterwards the Davidic King disappears and for the ensuing centuries the Jews are ruled by the High Priest alone.

Zachariah 14 concludes the book with the description of a great battle, usually understood to be the same final war described in Ezekiel. This battle is predicted to take place at Megiddo, called in Greek, Armageddon. Megiddo is a city in the Jezreel Valley, a level pass between the hill regions of Samaria and the Galilee in the Land of Israel. The ancient road from Egypt to Mesopotamia passed through this valley. Many great battles between the superpowers of Egypt and Assyria or Babylon took place in this central location. In apocalyptic speculation, Armageddon became the name for the final battle between the armies of God and the forces of evil.

Towards the end of the Second Temple era apocalyptic beliefs become extremely popular in Judea. Jews express their frustration with Roman cruelty and their own corrupt leaders with an apocalyptic hope that God will bring an end to time as we know it and institute a new era of direct divine rule over the earth, with a position of glory and sovereignty for the Jewish kingdom of Judea. There were many apocalyptic preachers in that era. Jesus of Nazareth was himself such an apocalyptic preacher, as Albert Schweitzer convincingly argues, though that message was later transformed into the doctrine of the Christ.

Apocalyptic literature proliferated. This body of literature was rejected by the early rabbis and lost to Judaism, but much of it was preserved by the Church.

The final book of the Christian New Testament is an apocalyptic work, John the Apocalypse (no relationship to the John who wrote the fourth Gospel). Historical scholars have debated whether this work is Christian or Jewish in origin, though it is certainly Christian in its current form. It is my opinion that the editors of the Apocalypse of John took an originally Jewish apocalyptic work and added in Christian portions.

**The End-Times Vision in Christianity and Judaism**

In apocalyptic belief, the time clock of history was set from the very beginning. Time is divided into eras based on the Sabbath. Historical time from Creation to Armageddon lasts for six thousand years, a week of millennia. The seventh, Sabbatical millennium is the era of Messianic rule over the earth. Apocalyptic Protestant Christianity of the type which arose in America in the 19th Century is often called Millennialism because of this time concept. There are many varieties of Christian Millennialism with a rich vocabulary of concepts. We will not attempt to sort all of this out. Rather, we describe the phenomenon in general terms.

The Era of the Messiah is initiated by a time of great troubles. Many humans will suffer and many will die. Some Christians believe in the Rapture, in which an elect few will be raised up to heaven so as not to suffer in the time of troubles. Raptured

219

individuals will be returned to earth after the triumph of the Messiah.

In Jewish apocalypticism there are two messiahs. The Messiah son of Joseph will fight God's wars during the time of troubles. In the decisive final battle, the Messiah son of Joseph will die. The Messiah son of David will then appear to lead God's forces to victory and rule over the world in the final millennium. After this comes the indescribable World-to-Come. The concept of the Messiah son of Joseph did not yet exist in the First Century, and so plays no role in the development of Christianity.

In Christian apocalypticism, the Jewish people have been preserved by God as witnesses to the Second Coming of Christ. In the final battles, all Jews will die except for a set number – perhaps 40,000. Those Jews will observe the Second Coming of Christ, who will arrive to win the final battle and rule over the world in the final millennium. Those surviving Jews will then become Christians. This realm of speculation has caused many apocalyptic Christians to support the modern State of Israel, which they see as ushering in the Final Days. Some Jews reject this support, which is based on a vision of the death or conversion of all the Jews. Many Jews welcome this support, since Jews appreciate the political support on the real-world level and do not believe in the apocalyptic predictions.

The Second Coming of Christ is not all that different in many respects from the Jewish hope for the Messiah. The Jewish Messiah is a flesh and blood human being, while Christ is divine, but the role of the Messiah and of the Christ of the Second Coming is similar – to punish evil, bring the reign of God's justice over the earth, and rule over a peaceful and united world.

A Jew might ask at this point – isn't the belief in the Second Coming in contradiction to the role of the divine Christ as defined by Paul? If the Christ fulfills his role by returning to Heaven so that those who believe in him may be saved, how does that conform with Jesus' role in the Second Coming? This is in some ways parallel to the paradox of belief in resurrection and in the eternal human soul. We have seen by now that religion is not greatly troubled by paradox. We can live with the contradictions. One might even say that the capacity to grasp both horns of a dilemma is a power of the religious mind.

## Apocalyptic and anti-Apocalyptic Religion in Christianity and Judaism

The earliest Christians expected the Second Coming of Christ to occur almost immediately, within the lifetime of every believer. When Christians began to die and Jesus had not yet returned, early Christianity had to answer new questions about what would become of the souls of those persons. Christianity easily adjusted to the delay of the *Parousia,* Christ's triumphant return. The Church established an organizational hierarchy and a set of beliefs and practices for the long run. At the same time, Christianity maintained a hope for the Second Coming. Movements like the Millennialist Protestantism of our own time arose periodically, with a focus on the immanence of the End-time.

Around the same time as the beginning of Christianity, the Jews of Judea fought a disastrous rebellion against the Roman Empire, 66-70 CE. We do not know if the rebels had any practical hope to defeat the mighty Romans, but many of the rebels were no doubt inspired by the apocalyptic belief that if the Jews started the war, they would force God's hand to intervene in history and save the Jews. That did not happen. The early rabbis strove to suppress apocalyptic beliefs which had led to such disaster for the Jews. Yohanan ben Zakkai, the Jewish leader after the rebellion, said, "If you are planting a tree and you hear that the Messiah has come, continue planting

221

the tree." (Avot d'Rabbi Natan 31b) Only a generation later, a new round of Jewish apocalypticism arose in desperate response to Emperor Hadrian's plan to rebuild Jerusalem as a pagan city. Rabbi Akiva gave the leader of a new rebellion, Simon bar Kochba, his official sanction as the Messiah. The result was another disaster for the Jews in 132-5 CE. The Jews renamed *bar Kochba*, "the star" as *bar Kozba*, "the liar." His actual name was bar Kosiba.

Periodically through history new messianic movements have arisen amongst the Jews. When Spain expelled the Jews in 1492 the leader of all Spanish Jewry, Isaac Abravanel, wrote three books predicting the imminent end of time. Each time his prediction was not fulfilled he wrote a new book. In 1665 a majority of the world's Jews believed in Shabbetai Zevi, the Kabbalistic messiah. They were disappointed in 1666 when Shabbetai was arrested by the Turkish Sultan and he converted to Islam to save his life.

Cycles of messianic fervor have characterized both Christianity and Judaism – and Islam as well. We could say that Judaism and Christianity together exist in two forms, the apocalyptic and the anti-apocalyptic. The apocalyptic forces believe that humankind must prepare for an imminent end-time in which only the righteous, believing few will survive. The anti-apocalyptic forces believe that humankind must act responsibly in expectation of a long residence on this earth in its present form. Apocalyptic believers welcome catastrophe in the expectation that God will save us from ourselves. The anti-apocalyptic forces believe that God has given humankind the capacity to maintain and improve life on earth, if we will faithfully follow God's will.

The anti-apocalyptic view is expressed in a Jewish teaching in which God gives the newly created Adam a tour of the earth. "Take good care of this world," God says to Adam, "Because if you ruin it there will be no one after you to repair it." (Kohelet Rabbah 1 on Ecclesiastes 7:13).

# CHAPTER TWENTY-EIGHT: THE DIVINE FEMININE

## Female Divine Imagery

Monotheism reduces the number of deities to one. That one God is represented in imagery that is overwhelmingly masculine. God is the Father. Jesus is undeniably male. The most common mental picture of God in monotheism is an old man with a long gray beard, sitting on a throne. The unitary God of monotheism in theory encompasses all opposites, including male and female. In theory, God is both. Despite this, the imagery through which humans think about God is overwhelmingly masculine.

Polytheistic religions have a multitude of deities, some of whom are female. It is simpler to represent the divine feminine in polytheism. Could we rediscover the divine feminine by returning to the old religions? The feminist appeal of ancient polytheistic religions may be exaggerated. In Mediterranean and Ancient Near Eastern religions the female deities constitute a "big three". There is a modest mother goddess, the "queen" (Juno, Hera). There is a sexy fertility goddess (Venus, Aphrodite, Ashtoret). There is a ferocious goddess (Diana, Artemis, Anat). Do these goddesses represent strong female role models for human society, or are they projections of male stereotypes about women, generated by a patriarchal society? Polytheism and monotheism both in the end reflect the male domination of society since the rise of civilization ten thousand years ago. Archeologists uncover a multitude of prehistoric female statuettes with exaggerated feminine features. Are these symbols of a prehistoric goddess religion, reflecting a matriarchal society, as some would like to believe, or are they ancient erotica? The statuettes are open to interpretation.

The demand for equality of women in our contemporary society has led to a desire among many persons to discover or

224

create strong feminine imagery in our theology and our worship. How can we accomplish this and remain monotheistic? That is a challenge that confronts Christianity and Judaism in our time. We recognize also that there are religious traditionalists in both religions who are content with masculine imagery for God and who may oppose attempts at egalitarian transformation.

## Catholic Reverence for Mary

In Catholic Christianity, the divine feminine is represented through reverence for Mary, the mother of Jesus. In Catholic belief, Mary was born without the taint of original sin. This is the "immaculate conception", a term which Jews often incorrectly think refers to virgin birth. Mary's sinless state made her the ideal vessel to be impregnated by the Holy Spirit, though she was a virgin. In Catholic belief, Mary remained a virgin her whole life, even after the birth of Jesus. Her betrothed, Joseph, supported her but did not reside with her. At the end of her life Mary did not die. She went to sleep and was transported to heaven. There is a Church of the Dormition on Mount Zion in Jerusalem, where this is believed to have taken place.

Reverence for a pure and compassionate virgin woman who is the mother of God incarnate is surely one of the attractions of Christianity through the ages. Mary is not included in the Holy Trinity, but reverence for her approaches that level. The New Testament requires that prayers, to be received on high, must be addressed to Jesus. Catholic and Orthodox Christianity provide that prayers may be addressed to saints, as intermediaries who will bring those prayers to Jesus. Catholics believe that prayers addressed to Mary have particular power, for through her compassion, which was only increased by enduring the tortured death of her son, Mary will surely receive prayers and bring them to God's attention. There are many

Sabbath Eve is her wedding ceremony. "Come and let us welcome the bride, the Sabbath" the worshipers sing.

I was once given a tour of a certain Catholic seminary by the spiritual director. We came to a lovely garden pond overlooked by a large statue of Mary. This insightful priest was certainly aware of how a Jew, a rabbi, would view a statue of a holy being. He said to me, "This garden is where we come to contemplate the divine feminine – you know, the Shechinah." His translation of his Catholic devotion into Jewish terms helped me understand the inner experience of the Catholic Christian in revering the Virgin Mary.

**Protestantism and Mary**

Orthodox Christians, Anglicans and Lutherans revere Mary, though not to the extent of Catholics. Other Protestants do not revere Mary. Many Protestants denounce reverence for Mary as a form of idolatry, which they call Mariolatry. Their objection is based in part on the belief that prayers should be addressed to God only through Jesus, and not through Mary nor any saint. They also object to the physical representation of Mary in statues. When you are walking down the street and you see a home with a little Mary shrine in the garden, that is almost certainly a Catholic home and not a Protestant home.

Protestants also object that many of the beliefs about Mary do not have biblical support. The New Testament often mentions Jesus' siblings. James, the brother of Jesus, was the leader of the Jerusalem Jewish Church that was opposed to Paul's Gentile Church. Catholics believe that Mary was a lifelong virgin, and the brothers and sisters of Jesus are in fact cousins. They argue that in First Century Judaism it was not unusual to address members of the extended family as brothers and sisters. Protestants take the New Testament at its word. They say that while Mary may have been a virgin at the time of Jesus' birth, she and Joseph then married and had sons and daughters. This is an object of contention between Protestants and Catholics.

## Conclusion

In modern America, as men and women stand together as social equals, how do we represent that equality in our address to God? How do we remain true to our monotheism and our traditions while recognizing that women, like men, require divine imagery that reminds them of their own selves? Within the bounds of the English language, how do recognize that God encompasses both the masculine and the feminine principles that permeate the cosmos of God's creation? How do we do this without sounding as if we are addressing two deities, one male and one female? How do we balance the egalitarianism of our society with the admittedly patriarchal and male dominated religious traditions we have inherited from the past? The resolution to these challenges lies in the future.

# CHAPTER TWENTY-NINE: HOW SHOULD CHRISTIANS ADDRESS JEWS?

"So many religions were represented at the interfaith gathering. There were Christians, Muslims, Hindus, Sikhs, and Jewish people." We might hear a sentence like this anywhere and any time in America. Our Christian neighbors are so uncomfortable saying the word "Jews" that they say "Jewish people" instead. Our good neighbors are trying hard not to offend. Their fear of saying the word "Jews" is well placed, considering the history of that word in American discourse.

When German Jews began arriving in America in large numbers in the 1840's, they came to a land where the word "Jew" was a dirty word in the English language. Persons called one another "Jew" as a pejorative, and accepted as obvious truths the most awful prejudices against Jews. It is still not rare to hear hard bargaining over a price called "Jewing" the price down.

Rather than fight the harsh meaning of the word "Jew", German Jewish immigrants adopted for themselves a term which had gentler connotations in the English language. They called themselves Israelites, or Hebrews. When Rabbi Isaac Mayer Wise organized the Reform Movement of Judaism in America in the 1880's, he called his movement the Union of American Hebrew Congregations. He called his seminary the Hebrew Union College. To this day, Jews in the U.S. military have Hebrew stamped on their dog tags for religion.

Friedrich Hegel, the German philosopher, was the father of the modern study of history. He shared the hatred towards Jews that was not uncommon in mid-19th Century Germany. In his historical writing Hegel used the term Hebrews to distinguish the pre-Christians whom he revered from the post-Christian Jews whom he despised. In the Hegelian dialectic, Judaism was replaced by Christianity, after which the Jews became zombies of history, refusing to recognize that they no longer existed. The term Hebrew exists in the Bible but is used only in the patriarchal era, and only when the patriarchs are identifying themselves to foreigners. By the time the tribes became a nation they were known as Israelites – literally, Children of Israel. After the Persian Empire arose, they were known as Jews. In the 19th Century, the term Hebrew was revived and became a synonym for Jew.

The German Jews chose to switch rather than fight. "If you hate Jews but love Hebrews", they more or less said to their Christian neighbors, "then we shall be Hebrews." It is also in this era that Zionist Jews began to call the Jewish language "Hebrew". The intention was to draw attention to the ancient roots of the language, which Jews formerly called the Holy Tongue.

The term Hebrew for Jews had its time and place, but that terminology has become quaint and outmoded. Most Jews of today would not know what to make of being called a Hebrew.

When Eastern European Jews began arriving on American shores after 1881, they were more numerous and more self-affirming. They came from close Jewish communities where the attitudes of their non-Jewish neighbors little affected them in their daily life. The East European Jews called themselves Jews without self-consciousness. They called their preferred rabbinical school the Jewish Theological Seminary. Since American Jews have long since reclaimed the word "Jew", it is acceptable for Christians to say "Jews". They do not have to say "Jewish people." This may require some additional training. We Jews can tell our Christian neighbors that it is okay to call us Jews. The East European Jews spoke a language called Yiddish, which means Jewish. The word for Jew in the Yiddish language is Yid. Yid is not a pejorative, though the word is little used today.

231

Israel was formerly a term for the collective of the Jewish people. That is the what "Israel" means in the Jewish prayer book. It is not a reference to a country but to a people. That is one reason the Jewish Agency chose in 1947 to name the country Israel, to identify that country with the collective of the Jewish people. Then language required a new name for Jews who are actually citizens of the country, as opposed to those who are not. That new word is "Israeli". An Israelite lived in ancient Israel. An Israeli lives in contemporary Israel. A Jew comes from the Land of Israel two thousand years ago, and may live in Israel or anywhere in the world today.

Most ethnic Americans adopt a hyphen. There are Irish-Americans, African-Americans, Italian-Americans, and so forth. Jews were the only ethnic Americans who put the American first, calling themselves American Jews. This distinction probably represents a degree of minority group self-consciousness on the part of Jews. They were anxious about being accepted as fellow Americans. Accusations of dual loyalty pointed at Jews, for example when they stand up for Israel, are still all too common. It may be time for Jewish-Americans to place their ethnicity before the hyphen like all the other proud ethnic groups who together make up the American people.

The biblical name for God is four Hebrew letters – yud, heh, vav, heh. No one knows how this name was pronounced in ancient Israel. Jews do not pronounce the Name, substituting the Hebrew for "Lord", "*Adonai*." In college and seminary classes on biblical history, Christian students are often told that the ancient Jews called God "*Yahweh*". This is a guess, based on the theory that the four-letter name is a causative form of the verb "to be", thus having the sense of "Creator of all." If any Israelites did call God Yahweh, that was a very long time ago. Many students come away from their class on biblical history believing that Jews even to this day call God Yahweh.

232

They may say "Yahweh" to Jews as a mark of friendly identification, often to the confusion of their Jewish friend. Clergy friends have often said to me, "Hey, Stephen, how is Yahweh treating you these days?" Jews should not be insulted by the use of Yahweh in address to us. It is intended to be friendly. It is okay to gently let our Christian friends know that we speak English, and we call God "God."

# CHAPTER THIRTY: THE BAD NEWS IN CHRISTIAN-JEWISH RELATIONS

## Has Christianity been Good or Bad for the Jews?

Some Jews believe that the Jewish people would have been better off if Christianity had not come into existence, considering all the persecution that Jews have suffered in the realms of Christendom. I do not share that assessment. A Judaism without Christianity is impossible to imagine, since Jews have lived in a Christian milieu through all but the formative years of our existence. The Jewish focus on Christian persecution is in part due to the fact that we have only recently experienced the Holocaust, the worst persecution in our history, and for that matter the history of all humankind. Naturally we see our past in the light of this genocide which took place across the entire span of the Christian world. Another reason we remember persecution is that Jewish theology encourages us to dwell on our sufferings because of their redemptive value. When we have suffered our full cup of suffering, according to traditional Jewish belief, then God will send the Messiah. And so, we say to God, "Look at us suffering! Now is the time!" The great Jewish historian, Salo Baron, warned against what he called "the lachrymose interpretation of Jewish history." The Jews are not some uniquely stubborn and defiant nation who continue to exist just to spite our enemies. No, the Jews still exist because in most times and most places it was good to be a Jew, as it is in America or Israel in our times. We also focus on our suffering at the hands of Christians because there has been a lot of bad, which we will confront directly in the next two chapters of this book.

Our sufferings should not blind us to the fact that while Christians often persecuted Jews, they more often protected Jews. Jews were the only tolerated minority group in a premodern world where minorities and dissidents were not tolerated. Jews were granted the protection of the Church, and many persecutions that Jews suffered, we suffered despite attempts by the Church leadership to protect us. There were many times and places where Jews and Christians got along quite well. Jews were considered desirable residents in Christian countries because of the prosperity we brought, which benefited all. Despite being foreigners – people from the country of Judah – Jews were welcomed into every land where we lived. The exception was Russia, the Czarist Empire, which acquired Jews by conquest despite never permitting Jews to live in Russia. Even there, the Jewish people thrived for some centuries.

Charlemagne (d.814) established the feudal system in Europe on the twin bases of land and Christianity. The feudal system needed outsiders to maintain trade, commerce, manufacture and finance. Charlemagne assigned Jews to this role. For centuries Jews were the sole traders in Christian lands, from international trade in commodities to the local sale of pots and sewing needles. Jews were the sole bankers in Christian lands. The Jewish monopoly on finance and trade lasted until the 15th Century, when Venice and Genoa began to take over those functions within the Christian world. When Jews were pushed out of our traditional functions in Western and Central Europe, we moved our center to the Christian lands of Eastern Europe, especially Poland, where Jews continued in their middle-man role until the dawn of modern times. Shakespeare's play *The Merchant of Venice* must be understood in light of the disappearance of the economic role of the Jew in Western Europe in Shakespeare's time. When Christians took over trade and banking the Jews became dispensable, and so were held in contempt.

The role assigned the Jews by Charlemagne gave Jews the opportunity to make a good living without working too hard.

This enabled Jews to pursue higher education in vast numbers, which was the highest Jewish value. It is often difficult for Americans to understand how Jews can be a persecuted people when we are doing so well economically. It was the peculiarity of the Jewish situation that we were held in contempt but granted a vital economic role near the top of the ladder of opportunity. Jews were not allowed to own land or work land; these roles were reserved by feudalism for Christians alone. Jews may have felt the sting of exclusion, but Jews did not have to do the back-breaking labor of the peasant farmer. Nobles and kings preferred to hire Jews to run their estates and the various franchises of their estates, such as milling and distilling. The *arrendar* was the Jewish estate manager, a very high and responsible position. The arrendar often served as *shtadlan*, an intermediary between the Jewish community and the Christian nobility.

There was some debate in feudal Christendom over the status of Jews. Those who looked down on Jews called us lower than serfs, because we could not live on the land. The Jews claimed a status equal to knights, because Jews had freedom of movement which was granted in feudal society only to those of knight class and above. All in all, Jews were better off than many of our neighbors. We must also remember that some eras of widespread death for Jews were also eras of widespread death for Christians and Muslims. Life could be hard in the premodern world.

**Persecutions**

When the Roman Empire became officially Christian, they passed laws meant to limit the spread of Judaism and give Christianity an advantage. Jews were prohibited from holding public office which would give them authority over Christians. Jews were prohibited from building new synagogues, though they were permitted to repair old ones. Jews were prohibited from converting anyone to Judaism, under pain of death for both the convert and the Jew.

Ultimately the Church determined the status of the Jew in Christendom. Jews were protected in life and property, but were to be held in contempt and subjugated, as a public example of what happens to people who refuse to become Christian. Jews are recognized as the Chosen People of the Old Testament, whose covenant with God has been replaced and succeeded by the New Covenant of Christ. It was prohibited to forcibly convert any Jew to Christianity, but Jews were to be encouraged to convert in both attractive and punitive ways. Any Jew who became a Christian immediately lost Jewish status and was welcomed into the Christian fold.

The various disabilities placed upon the Jews should be understood in terms of the times. Only in modern times has tolerance of national, racial and religious minorities been seen as a virtue. Conformity was prized in ancient and Medieval societies. The Jews were the only officially tolerated minority in the Christian world. This becomes significant after the French Revolution, where the question of the status of the Jews was raised anew. The Jews had been set apart for two millennia. What now? This issue became known as The Jewish Question. When Hitler decided to kill all the Jews he called this the Final Solution to the Jewish Question.

It is not clear to what extent the legal disabilities of the Jewish people were enforced. Most likely they were overlooked in times and places when Jews and their neighbors had good relations, and were enforced when it suited the rulers of the time. Local custom predominated everywhere, with the result that there were many places where Jews owned land and farmed, for example.

## In the Middle Ages

England had no exceptions to the rules about Jews. There were no Jews in England until they were imported by William the Conquerer after 1066. William reformed England as a perfect feudal society. Jews were restricted to the one profession of money-lending. In Europe, Jews may have owed fealty to a local nobleman, but in England all Jews were the King's men. This gave the King control of the banking system. He alone set interest rates and taxed the profits on loans. Control of the Jews gave the King advantage over his barons, who had no Jews of their own. As the English barons gained power relative to the King (think of the *Magna Carta*), the Jews became a bargaining chip.

In the High Middle Ages, prejudice against the Jews increased. Papal decrees placed limits on Jewish life and activity. The Fourth Lateran Council of 1215 under Pope Innocent III required Jews to wear special clothing, including a conical hat, and a yellow badge on their clothing. The Nazi yellow badge, and the Nazi Nuremberg laws against the Jews, were a restoration of the persecution laws of the Medieval Church. As in earlier times, the enforcement of these laws varied and depended upon local conditions.

The city of Venice decreed in 1516 that all Jews must live in a certain section of the city which was surrounded by a wall. The gate in the wall would be closed and locked at night from the outside. The Jewish section was called the Ghetto, after an iron-works, the Gioto, which was in the neighborhood. This is the origin of the term ghetto. It became customary throughout central Europe, in the German states and Italy, for Jews to live in ghettos. The ghetto was first welcomed by the Jews. It was usual in the Middle Ages for people to live in walled communities. As time went by the ghetto became crowded and unsanitary, and the Jews were more and more cut off from the world around them. The ghetto became a tool of segregation and persecution. When Napoleon conquered the German and Italian states in the late 18th and early 19th centuries, he tore down the ghetto walls everywhere. Napoleon was defeated in 1815, but the Jews could not be forced back into the ghetto. This was the sudden entry into modernity for a large number of Jews.

The establishment of the preaching orders of monks in the Medieval Catholic Church led to new persecutions of the Jews. The Dominican and Franciscan friars of the 13th Century traveled through Europe, promoting a new religious devotion amongst the faithful. Anti-Judaism was unfortunately a part of the message. The masses were inflamed against the Jews by the new preaching, and there was a renewed effort to convert the Jews.

## Disputations

This renewed religious spirit in the Christian world led to the era of Disputations, where Jews were forced to present a scholar to engage in public debate with a Christian scholar. The disputations generally centered on whether the messianically understood verses in the Hebrew Bible refer to the Christ or to the Jewish messiah. The terms of the disputations were highly disadvantageous to the Jews, who were not permitted to say anything that would insult Christianity. The disputant rabbis had to uphold the honor of Judaism and the safety of their community while showing deference to the Christian scholars and the nobles or royals who sponsored the disputation.

Christian scholars studied Judaism to find material to bring against the Jews from their own sources in the disputations. Christians became aware of the Talmud and of rabbinic literature. This led to some question as to whether the Jews should really be tolerated as the people of the Old Testament, since Jews like Christians had additional later Scriptures.

Two of the most famous disputations are the Disputation of Paris in 1240, sponsored by the Queen Mother Blanche, and the Disputation of Barcelona in 1263, sponsored by King James of Aragon. In both cases the Christian disputant was a Jew who had converted to Christianity and so was conversant with Jewish teachings. In the Disputation of Paris, the Talmud was placed on trial. Isaac Donin debated with Rabbi Yehiel of Paris and others leading French rabbis. In the Disputation of Barcelona, the Christian disputant, Pablo Christiani, used texts from the midrash, fanciful rabbinical interpretation of the Bible, to prove that Jesus is the Jewish messiah. The Jewish disputant, Moses Nahmanides, was not prepared for this line of argument. He did not fare well. In shame, he departed Spain and lived out his days in the land of Israel. There were numerous additional disputations, some of international fame and others of local import.

**Crusades and Black Death**

Many historical scholars believe that the disaster brought on the Jews by the Crusades may have been exaggerated by earlier historians. The heart-breaking poetry composed by survivors of persecuted communities may have created the impression that massacres of Jews were widespread. The Crusades, which began in 1095, were aimed not against the Jews but against the Muslim rulers of the Holy Land. Popes generally reminded the Crusaders that the Jews were a protected people. The religion passion aroused by the Crusades occasionally caused riots against the local "infidels", the Jews. There were massacres of Jews in the Rhineland in 1096, in Mainz and Worms, and the Crusaders massacred all the Jews of Jerusalem when they conquered the city in 1099. The rampaging Crusaders in Jerusalem also killed all the Muslims of the city and all the non-Catholic Christians. The Jewish communities of the Rhineland and of Jerusalem were reconstituted shortly thereafter.

Many more Jews were killed during the Black Death of 1347-51. The Black Death was a virulent outbreak of the Plague, so named because victim's faces turned black as they were dying. A third to a half of the entire population of Europe died in the Black Death. Whole regions became unpopulated and returned to forest for a century and more. The panicked Christian population of Europe looked for a cause of the devastation. Many believed that God may be angry with them for tolerating the presence of unbelievers in their midst. Massacres of Jews ensued in many locales. In Strasbourg on St. Valentine's Day in 1349 hundreds of Jews were herded onto a wooden platform and burned alive.

It is a common myth amongst contemporary Jews that Jewish hygiene laws prevented Jews from getting the Plague, thus causing suspicion among Christians that Jews were causing the disease by poisoning wells. Historians have established that Jews died from the Plague at the same rate as their Christian neighbors. This did nothing to dispel suspicion in the atmosphere of panic and fear. We may note that even in our times, when the natural causes of disease are well established, the outbreak of a new pandemic, such as AIDS or Covid19, has led to the scapegoating of feared minorities.

It is interesting to note that the widespread mortality during the Black Death led to a reimagining of one of the best-known figures in Jewish and Christian mythology, the Angel of Death. The Angel of Death had always been depicted as carrying a sword, with which he picked off those persons whose time had come. In the Black Death the sword was replaced with a scythe, which mows people down en masse. This image has persisted.

**The Era of Expulsions**

We have emphasized that in many times and places, Jews and Christians lived side by side in peace, with Jews fulfilling the role assigned them by society. The era of expulsions was a time of great tragedy for the Jews. This era began in 1290 with the expulsion of Jews from England and concluded with the expulsion of Jews from Spain in 1492 and the mass forced conversion of the Jews of Portugal in 1497. In the interim, Jews were expelled, region by region, from most of the realms of France and Germany. After the expulsions, Jews were gone from most of Western Europe for centuries. Multitudes of Jews died attempting to relocate, or converted in despair. The survivors of the Spanish expulsion reconstituted their communities in the Turkish Empire, in North Africa, in the Netherlands, and in some Italian city-states which welcomed Jewish refugees. Ashkenazic Jews from Franco-Germany were welcomed into the emerging Kingdom of Poland and Lithuania, which from the 16th Century on became the new world center of Jewry. The remnant communities were just a few sparks pulled from the ashes of a great conflagration.

In England in 1190 there were anti-Jewish riots that spread from the south to the north. In York the Jewish community were cornered in the fortified Tower of York. The Jews committed mass suicide, with the remainder burned alive in the Tower or murdered by the mob. Richard the Lionheart was King of England and a renowned Crusader. In 1192, during his return from the Holy Land, Richard was captured and imprisoned by the Duke of Austria, who held him for ransom. This was a common practice amongst the Christian nobility of the Middle Ages, but never before had a king been captured. The ransom of three million silver marks was collected from the Jews of England, who were given six months to turn over the money "or else". The ransom impoverished the Jews, which made them less valuable to the king. In 1290 King Edward I issued an edict of expulsion against all the Jews of England.

242

Spain was, for centuries, the world center of Jewry. After the Muslim conquest of Spain in 711 the country was divided between a Muslim south and a Christian north. The Jews of Spain are called Sephardic, to distinguish them from the Jews of European Christendom who are called Ashkenazic. During the centuries of the Christian Reconquista the border between Christian and Muslim rule gradually shifted southward. The need for Muslims and Christians to coexist in Spain led to an era of interfaith tolerance unusual for the times. Jews thrived in this atmosphere. Also, as Muslims and Christians vied for power, each group benefited by having Jews on their side. Spain was the wealthiest country on earth, and Christians, Muslims and Jews all lived well for a time. The good times came to an end with the completion of the Reconquista and the imposition of the Inquisition in Spain to root out heresy.

In 1391 there were anti-Jewish riots throughout Spain. About half of Spain's large Jewish community converted to Christianity to save their lives. After their conversion they were legally Christians, but in the lax atmosphere of Spain they continued to identify as Jews. They were required by law to attend church on Sunday but they did not participate in the worship. These lax Christians were surprised a century later when the Inquisition was imposed and they found themselves obligated to observe Christianity strictly, at cost of their property and their life.

In 1492 King Ferdinand and Queen Isabella of Spain conquered Granada, the last Muslim kingdom in the Spanish peninsula. They issued an Edict of Expulsion against all Muslims and Jews in Spain. The date set for Jews to depart from Spain was the 9th day of the month of Av, the Jewish day of sorrows on which both the First and Second Jerusalem Temples were burned. As Columbus sailed, he passed Jews climbing on board ships to depart from Spain. Multitudes of Jews converted rather than leave their beloved Spain. Many of the more devout Jews went to Portugal, where they were forcibly converted a few years later.

Jews tend to exaggerate the Jewish devotion of the Marranos, the secret Jews of Spain. Most conversos lived as Catholics until they were persecuted as Jews. A half million Jews became Catholics and suddenly had no barriers to their rise in society. Old Catholics felt greatly threatened by the competition. They developed a racial conception of the Jew like that we associate with modern anti-Semitism. The New Christians were held suspect and often denounced to the Inquisition. Most Marranos who reverted to Judaism did so in response to persecution by Old Catholics. By this time there were no more Jews in Spain to teach them about their ancestral religion. Secret Jews more or less invented their own religion out of Old Testament readings and family memories. The Inquisition tortured suspected secret Jews to extract confessions. The Inquisition acquired the property of all convicts, so they had selfish reasons to find people guilty of heresy. Most people confess under torture to whatever they think will stop the pain. Those convicted of a second offense were sentenced to burning. If they confessed to Christianity at the stake they were strangled before burning. If they insisted on dying as Jews, they were burned alive.

There were more secret Jews in Portugal, where the Jewish community had been forcibly converted. Over the course of time the number of secret Jews diminished. The most determined Jews attempted escape. Many of these ended up in Amsterdam, a Protestant city which was fighting its own war against the Catholic rulers of Spain. The Jews who escaped to freedom were often surprised to discover the true nature of Judaism. It was different from the Judaized Catholicism that they had come to practice in Spain and Portugal. Secret Jews also escaped to southern France and to England, where they quietly reverted to Judaism under the benign eye of the local authorities. In this way Jewish communities were reestablished in these countries. The Edict of Expulsion was never revoked in England, with the happy result that with the coming of the Enlightenment no laws were passed limiting the citizenship rights of English Jews, as happened in Germany and other places. Oliver Cromwell, leader of the Roundheads in the English Civil War of 1642-51, welcomed Jews back to England in the belief that this would hasten the Second Coming of Christ, which according to the Bible required that Jews be returned to their homeland in Israel "from the far corners of the earth."

Many secret Jews attempted to escape the Inquisition by moving to the Spanish territories in the New World. The Inquisition followed them to Mexico or Peru, and many were captured. It is an oddity of our times that many Central American Christians choose to consider themselves to be descendants of secret Jews. This is usually not accompanied by any desire to return to Judaism; it has rather to do with pride in descent. Historical researchers have debunked these claims, which mostly are made without evidence. People have family stories of a grandmother who lit candles in the cellar on Friday night without knowing why. It may be that some of these people had a Jewish ancestor. For the most part the conversos of Spain and Portugal merged into Christian society over the generations. The depredations of the Inquisition and the Iberian focus on limpieza, blood purity, damaged Spain and helped end her status as a world power.

As the era of expulsions came to an end, the diminished Sephardic Jewish community was re-established in Amsterdam, London, the Provence, Italy, the Turkish Empire, and the Middle East. The now much larger Ashkenazic community became established in the Kingdom of Poland and Grand Duchy of Lithuania, which in the 1500's was the largest kingdom in Europe.

## The Chmielniki Massacres in Ukraine

Most Slavic peoples are Orthodox Christians. A notable exception are the Poles, who are Catholic Christians. In 1648 the Cossack leader Bogdan Chmielniki led a rebellion of the Orthodox Christian people of Ukraine against their Polish rulers. The Ukraine was at that time a region of the Polish kingdom. The Cossacks were warlike horse people of the steppes. From 1648-54 waves of Cossack fighters attacked and pushed out the Poles, establishing an Orthodox Christian kingdom of Ukraine, which ultimately fell under Russian rule.

The Cossack rebellion had the character of a religious war, even though both sides were Christian. As the Cossacks massacred the Catholic Poles, they also massacred the allies of the Poles, the Jews. Historians once estimated that 300,000 Jews were murdered by Chmielniki and his allies. Contemporary historians have revised that number downward to perhaps 50,000. No matter the exact number, it was the worst mass killing of Jews from the Roman wars of antiquity until the Holocaust. The Cossacks devised cruel tortures to amuse themselves in the murder of Jews. Jewish life in the Ukraine was devastated, opening the way for Jews to follow the false messiah Shabbetai Zevi and, eventually, for the rise of Hasidism, a revivalist movement which brought hope to the shattered and impoverished Jewish communities of the Ukraine.

Bogdan Chmielniki is looked upon by Ukrainians as their national liberator. There is an equestrian statue of him in the center of Kiev. Had Hitler won the Second World War, there would be a similar statue in his honor today in central Berlin.

## The Modern Era

In the time of the Enlightenment and the French Revolution the old religious anti-Judaism was succeeded by a new form of hatred against Jews, anti-Semitism. Anti-Semitism is hatred against Jews as a people. Though secular in nature, anti-Semitism drew upon the history of Christian anti-Judaism. The Jews are seen as a people apart. Anti-Semites were not restrained by any of the moral scruples of the Christian religion. This secular ideology proved far deadlier than religious hatred against the Jews.

The Russian Empire never welcomed Jews, but the conquests of the 18th Century brought millions of Jews under the rulership of the Czar. Jews were restricted to a region called the Pale of Settlement, including Poland, Lithuania, Ukraine, and White Russia. Policies were put in place to impoverish and oppress the Jews. The Russian plan to eliminate the Jews was that one third would be pushed into conversion, one third would be killed by starvation, death in military service and other means, and one third would emigrate.

Pogroms, organized riots against the Jews, became a regular feature of life in the Russian Empire. In 1903 the Kishinev Pogrom in the Moldova region led to the death of hundreds of Jews. It was a major uptick in anti-Jewish violence which was the first hint of the Holocaust to come.

That same year saw the publication of *The Protocols of the Elders of Zion*. This anti-Semitic tract was based on an earlier work intended to satirize the rule of Napoleon III of France. Now it was twisted into hate literature against the Jews. Though a modern work, it drew upon ancient prejudices against the Jews that were common in Christian lands. The work suggests that the Jews are a secret cabal who rule the world for their own benefit, using money and sex to control the world's leaders. Henry Ford, the auto magnate, paid to publish and spread this work in America, under the title *The International Jew*. In his later years Ford regretted his anti-Semitism and attempted to suppress the book. Hitler never accepted Ford's repentance, and he kept a photo of Henry Ford in his office. The *Protocols* has largely disappeared from the Christian world in our day. Sad to say, the work has found new life in the Muslim world, where national leaders have promoted the book as part of their program to foment hatred against the Jewish State of Israel. In America and in Germany there is some debate as to whether the book should be totally suppressed, or made available for the historical study of anti-Semitism.

We will not review here the whole tragic history of the Holocaust, the murder of six million Jews during the Second World War. Nazi ideology was not Christian; in many ways it was anti-Christian. Yet, Nazi anti-Semitism drew upon a history of two millennia of Christian anti-Judaism. The entire world of Christendom rose up to murder the Jews in their midst, from West to East. The Allies, Great Britain and the United States, participated in the Holocaust by closing their borders to Jewish immigration, by refusing to bomb the murder facilities, and by their diplomatic silence which Hitler took as encouragement and collusion. The Holocaust was not the work of one madman; it was the culmination of two thousand years of the teaching of hatred against the Jews.

In the wake of the Holocaust, it should be understood that the sincere repentance of many Christian denominations for their history of anti-Judaism, and also Christian support for the restoration of Jewish national sovereignty in the Land of Israel, are not to be seen as emotional reactions to the Holocaust. They are, rather, necessary corrections to historical wrongs, overdue but always welcomed.

We must keep in mind that it is not anti-Semitism that was defeated in 1945, but the German army. For some decades the horrors of Nazism and German imperialism made public expressions of anti-Semitism unpopular. Anti-Semitism went underground for a period of time but it did not disappear. In

248

our own times, a pretense of concern for the Palestinian people has restored a sheen of moral respectability to hatred against the Jews. We welcome genuine concern for the human rights of Palestinians, but such a concern, if sincere, would not be accompanied by the demonization of the Jewish state. The Zionist movement had as one goal that the "normalization" of Jewish nationality would bring an end to anti-Semitism. Instead, anti-Judaism and anti-Semitism have reestablished themselves as anti-Zionism. It is grievous to see some American Christian denominations formally adopt anti-Zionist platforms, reviving all the old canards against the Jews.

# CHAPTER THIRTY-ONE: THE BLOOD ACCUSATION

The deepest source of anti-Jewish prejudice in the Christian world is the accusation that the Jews have committed deicide. The Jews, it was said, have murdered God. The Jews were called "Christ-killers." This unfortunate attitude led in the Middle Ages to the accusation that Jews regularly perform the ritual murder of Christians as a reenactment of the murder of the Christ. The belief arose among Christians that Jews require the blood of a Christian child to make Passover matzoh. This is called "the blood libel" or "the blood accusation."

Our earliest known example of the blood accusation occurs in Norwich, England in the year 1144. A twelve-year-old boy, William of Norwich, was found murdered in the woods outside of the town. It was the Easter-Passover season. There are various theories about the cause of his death, but no one knows for sure. The Jewish community of Norwich were accused of ritual murder. A local cult of Saint William of Norwich followed, and the legend grew. In the following years, whenever a Christian child disappeared or was found murdered, Jews were accused of ritual murder. Hugh of Lincoln (1255) is a notable example. The blood libel spread from England to other nations.

A related accusation is that Jews would steal into a church in the middle of the night and stick pins into the consecrated host (the communion wafer) to make it bleed. The blood libel is probably related to the controversy in the Church at that time over "transubstantiation", the belief that during Holy Communion the wine and wafer turn into the actual blood and body of Christ. It is ludicrous on many levels to believe that Jews would stab a communion wafer and make it bleed, but for a Christian who is arguing passionately with other Christians in favor of transubstantiation, the blood accusation against the Jews lends credence to the religious belief.

Over the centuries there have been numerous blood libel cases against the Jews, often resulting in riots in which some Jews were killed. An angry mob could easily be aroused by such a case. It is likely that in some cases a child was murdered and his body planted in the Jewish part of town by instigators who desired a riot against the Jews for their own reasons – perhaps because they owed debts that they could not pay and desired to destroy the financial records of the Jews in a riot.

It seems futile to bring a rational defense against this hysterical and hateful accusation, but it is worth noting that Jews do not eat blood of any kind, not even that of kosher animals. Blood is prohibited in the kosher laws. The meat of a kosher animal must be salted and soaked before cooking to remove all blood, or else the meat must be broiled to cook out the blood.

The Damascus Blood Libel of 1840 is notable because, for the first time in history, a defense against the accusation was organized by both Christian and Jewish people who objected to such barbarism in the Age of Enlightenment. When a certain monk was killed in Damascus, then a part of the Turkish Empire, the local Jewish community were accused by the authorities of ritual murder. The authorities doubtless had their own motives for bringing the charge. Enlightened people all over Europe demanded justice for the Jews. In France, leading Jews formed the Alliance Israelite Universelle to fight the charges. The Alliance exists to this day as a league of leading French Jews and a defender of Jewish and human rights. The American President, Martin van Buren, ordered his diplomats to express American outrage at the charge. The case was dropped in response to the international pressure.

This did not bring an end to blood libel cases. The Mendel Beilis case in Kiev, Russian Empire, became quite famous in

1913. Beilis was accused by the government of the ritual murder of a certain child, though it was known that he had been killed by gangsters. The trial brought world-wide attention. Beilis was acquitted by a jury. The case seems to have been related to attempts by the Russian Czars to cling to power by turning the anger of the masses against the Jews. The Beilis case has been the subject of books and also of a renowned novel, *The Fixer*, by Bernard Malamud.

In the 21st Century the blood libel is actively propagated in many Muslim nations. Anti-Jewish teachings, many of which originated in Christian lands and were formerly absent in Muslim lands, have been fomented as part of the anti-Israel campaign to demonize Jews. It seems to be the strategy of opponents of Israel to further their cause by drilling into the wells of historic anti-Jewish hatred. This strategy was developed in the 1970's by the Soviet Union, the Palestinian Liberation Organization, and some Arab states. It seemed as if the easiest way to arouse sympathy for the Palestinian cause is to promote hatred against the Jewish people and the Jewish State. There is a continuity from anti-Judaism to anti-Semitism to anti-Zionism. Hard as it is to believe, there are Muslims in the world today who solemnly believe, as they have been taught, that Jews use the blood of Christian children to make Passover matzoh.

# CHAPTER THIRTY-TWO: IF JESUS WAS A JEW, HOW COULD ANY CHRISTIAN NOT LOVE US?

The title of this chapter is a question that Jews often pose to their rabbi. It seems to many Jews that if a Christian loves Jesus then a Christian must love the people of Jesus. To hate Jews is to hate Jesus, right? The question results from a misunderstanding of the way Christianity evolved out of its Jewish roots.

In fact, my Jewish friends, it is precisely the fact that Jesus was Jewish that has been held against us. It seems natural to many a believing Christian that all people should believe in Jesus. It is perhaps understandable that a person in some distant corner of the world may not be a Christian believer. Those people may not have heard about Jesus, except as a distant rumor, or the customs and religion of their own nation might make it difficult for them to hear the Good News. There is no excuse, though, for Jesus' own people to have rejected him as their Lord and Savior. To some Christians, this can only be interpreted as pure obstinacy or perversity. The Jews were called "perfidious", which means both untrustworthy and lacking in faith.

To a Christian person, Christ is the center of their religion. Many Christians imagine that Christ is equally at the center of the Jewish religion. It may seem to a Christian who does not know Judaism that as Christianity is all about accepting Christ, Judaism is all about rejecting Christ. It may be difficult for a Christian to understand that Jews really don't think about Jesus at all when we are practicing our religion and way of life. It may help to explain to a Christian friend that as much as they think about whether or not Mohammed is the final prophet of God, that is how much Jews think about Christ. That is, it's simply another religion altogether.

In the mind of many Christians, if you took Christianity and eliminated Christ, the part that is left over is Judaism. That would be a religion with a big Christ-shaped hole in the middle, just waiting to be filled by Jesus Christ. When some Christians think of Judaism in this way, no wonder it is difficult for them to imagine why Jews do not give up our stubborn resistance and become Christian.

When Christians ask me why I don't believe in Jesus, especially after all that I have studied about him, I do not try to explain to my Christian friend what I, as a Jew, think of Jesus. My to-the-point response is, "Judaism has the answers to all of my religious questions." To answer that Jews respect Jesus as a great teacher or a prophet is irrelevant to the question that is being asked. What my Christian friend needs to understand is, why am I not longing for Christ? The answer, which may be surprising to my friend, is that Judaism is a complete religion.

The fact that Jesus was Jewish may make a Christian angry at the Jews. Psychological rationales have been offered for this emotional reaction. A Christian must believe in Jesus to be saved. The Jews, Jesus' own people, do not believe him to be the Christ, the divine Savior. Perhaps Jewish unbelief fills some Christians with doubt. That doubt is dangerous and unacceptable, so it becomes easier to hate the Jews than deal with one's own doubts that may endanger one's salvation.

A Freudian interpretation is that Christians who love Jesus also harbor an unconscious hatred towards him. Jesus forces them to turn the other cheek, to love their enemies, to share their property with the less fortunate – to do many things that go against the darker side of human nature. Rather than admit that one has mixed feelings towards the Savior who makes one behave in all these unnatural ways, it resolves the unconscious conflict to transfer the anger onto Jesus' people, the Jews. Some interpreters have referred to the Freudian Oedipus

254

complex. Judaism is the father and Christianity is the child. The child has an unconscious urge to kill the father and take his place.

Psychological interpretations of anti-Jewish feeling among Christians are interesting to contemplate and may lead to some level of understanding, but they are not definitive. One cannot psychoanalyze over a billion people.

It is heartening that especially in the post-Holocaust era, and in light of modern historical study, a new appreciation of the Jewish roots of Jesus has arisen in many Christian circles. There are multitudes of Christians who are grateful to the Jewish people for establishing the basis of Christianity and for being the extended family of Jesus. There are Christian who believe that, to be better Christians, they need to get more in touch with the Jewish influence within Christianity. In our final chapter we will look at some of these positive trends in Christian-Jewish relations.

# CHAPTER THIRTY-THREE: WHY DID CHRISTIANITY AND NOT JUDAISM CONQUER THE WORLD?

This is the second big question that Jews constantly ask their rabbi. We are so few, and they are so many. Is that just a quirk of history, and if so, what caused it? Could it have been the other way around if history had unfolded differently?

The quick answer is "no." Judaism was not in competition to be a world religion. We Jews did not lose a contest that we never entered. Christianity and Islam were specifically designed to be the religion of many nations and peoples. Judaism was not.

The Sages of ancient Judaism saw Judaism as the way of life of a particular nation, the Jewish people. The Pharisees welcomed converts to Judaism, but those converts had to join the Jewish people to become a Jew. The convert was then no longer a member of his or her birth people. Jews lived by the laws of the Jewish people, observed the customs, measured the meaning of the days of the year by the Jewish calendar. Judaism demanded observances that seemed natural to a Jew but burdensome or off-putting to a non-Jew, particularly the kosher food laws and the circumcision of males. There were Gentiles in the ancient world who worshiped the one God of the Jews and kept the Sabbath and observed some Jewish rituals. Such persons were known as "God-fearers." The God-fearers were respected and welcomed, but were not considered Jews and did not think of themselves as Jews. Many of the ancient God-fearers may have ultimately joined Christianity. When Paul eliminated the obligation to keep kosher and to circumcise for Christians, he may have been reaching out to just such persons. Now they had a religion where they could worship the one God without having to become a Jew and live by the laws and rules of the Jewish nation. Christian converts could worship God while still belonging to the nation of their birth. Christianity separated religion from nationality and was highly adaptable to various cultures.

We have mentioned before the miracle, that in the 4th Century the entire Roman Empire abandoned the ancient religions and sought out a new religion. There was no chance that Judaism was going to be that religion – not with the demands that Judaism places upon the Jews, and not with the history of Jewish rebellion against the Empire. The amazing thing for Jews is that the Empire ultimately settled upon a religion with a remarkable amount of Jewish influence. That religion is Christianity. The people of the Empire could have chosen a religion, such as the once popular cults of Mithra or Isis, which had no relationship to Judaism. Instead, the Empire chose Christianity, a religion built around reverence for a Jewish person, Jesus of Nazareth, as a divine being, the Christ. In choosing Christianity, the Gentiles adopted the Jewish Holy Scriptures as their own. They adopted the Jewish moral code, centered upon the Ten Commandments. They adopted the seven-day week and took one day of every week as a day of rest and worship. This is a remarkable amount of influence for a small people descended from a single ancient tribe, the tribe of Judah from the tribal confederation of Israel. Perhaps the Jewish people survive to this day because we thrive on the attention of being so central to the religion of Christians. Judaism was also a strong influence on Islam. Worship five times a day, the prohibition of eating pork, the worship of one God, a seventh day of rest and worship, all these principles of Islam derive from Jewish influence.

We Jews should not feel bad that our religion did not become a world religion. We should feel proud that our religion has had so much influence upon the peoples of the world through the religions that drew upon the resources of Judaism, Christianity and Islam.

257

The Sages of old told a tale of three mountains. God did not give the Torah on Mr. Carmel, the most beautiful of mountains. Nor did God give the Torah on Mt. Hermon, the tallest of mountains. God gave the Torah on Mt. Sinai, a humble and undistinguished mountain. The legend is about the three monotheistic faiths. Christians are pleased by the earthly success of Christianity. Muslims take pride in the beautiful language of the Koran. Jews historically have neither power nor beauty, but we have an important role to play in the world as bearers of the Torah, witnesses to God's word and God's justice and mercy. If we Jews play our role well it matters not that we are few in number and relatively powerless.

# CHAPTER THIRTY-FOUR: CHRISTIAN-JEWISH RECONCILIATION

The past sixty years have seen a miraculous transformation in Christian-Jewish relations. There has been nothing like it in the preceding two millennia. There was a lot of silence after the Holocaust, from Jews as well as Christians. The world was in shock over what had been done. Twenty years after the end of the Second World War, just as the first Jewish literary and philosophical responses to the Holocaust came into print, the Christian world took action.

The Catholic Church led the way. In 1965, as part of the Pope John XXIII's Second Vatican Council to reform and update the Church, the Catholic Church published a statement on the Jews, named *Nostra Aetate*. The document affirmed the validity of Judaism in an ongoing Jewish covenant with God. Most important, *Nostra Aetate* stated that no Jews living in our times should be held responsible for the death of Jesus. Since Jesus died willingly and for the sake of Christian salvation, there should be no focus on assigning blame for his death. The Catholic Church in America responded enthusiastically to *Nostra Aetate* by expunging all anti-Jewish teachings from Catholic educational materials. A Catholic child growing up in the past few decades in America would not even know that the Jews had ever been accused of deicide. The Catholic Church in other nations was slower to respond, but the end result has been very positive.

There have been further developments in Catholic-Jewish relations. Pope John Paul II enthusiastically promoted a new and equal relationship between Christians and Jews. He visited the synagogue in Rome, the first Pope since antiquity to do so. He sat next to the rabbi on equal throne chairs, symbolically expressing that he sees the Jews as religious equals before God. The Vatican gave diplomatic recognition to the State of Israel.

This was a theological as well as political statement, indicating that the "old Israel of the flesh" has not been replaced by the "new Israel of the spirit." The two "Israels" may co-exist in relationship with God.

Good Friday was once a frightening day for Jews. The Good Friday liturgy once denounced the "perfidious Jews." Worshipers exited Church on Good Friday in a fury; Jews would lock themselves into their homes for safety on that day. Pope Pius XII directed the Catholic Church to drop the prayer about the "perfidious Jews." After the Second Vatican Council, the Church replaced it with a far more positive prayer: "Let us pray also for the Jewish people, to whom the Lord our God spoke first, that He may grant them to advance in love of His name and in faithfulness to His covenant."

Supersessionism, or "replacement theology", is the belief that Christianity replaced Judaism, leaving Judaism irrelevant and outside of God's plan after the time of Jesus. Many Christian churches have rejected supersessionism, validating that the Jewish covenant with God is for all time. Many Christians affirm that a Jew may enter heaven by being faithful to Judaism. The Catholic Church has stated that no special effort should be made to convert Jews to Christianity. This is still a touchy subject between Jews and Christians, as Jews would like all missionary efforts aimed at Jews to cease, while Christians see evangelism as essential to their faith.

Since *Nostra Aetate* many Protestant denominations have followed suit, issuing their own declarations of support for the validity of the Jewish religion and the Jewish people, renouncing anti-Jewish teachings and anti-Semitism. The Evangelical Lutheran Church of America formally repudiated Martin Luther's essay *On the Jews and their Lies*. It is beyond the scope of this book to list all the important documents that have been issued by Christian churches on the subject of Christian-Jewish relations, but they are many.

The State of Israel remains a sore point in Christian-Jewish relations, particularly within some liberal Protestant denominations. Many Christian liberals are happy to validate Jewish religion but not so Jewish peoplehood or sovereign rights. If the Jews are defined only as a religion then what right have they to a state? The fact that Jews have always recognized ourselves as a people, and Judaism as the religion of that people, is often overlooked or not understood. The principle of self-determination is not always applied to Jews. The claim that "Zionism is Racism", while grounded in baseless hatred, is given an intellectual rationale by the claim that Judaism is a religion only, and not the way of life of a nation. In the guise of a sometimes-sincere passion for social justice, Christian supporters of Palestinian rights have too often demonized Israel in classic anti-Semitic ways. The words "apartheid", "racist" and "colonialist" have replaced "Christ-killer" as terms to demonize Jews and give moral validation to Jew-hatred. Is it possible to criticize the State of Israel without being called an anti-Semite? Yes, but not if one uses anti-Semitic memes to denounce Israel, or if one correlates Israel with Nazism, or if one holds Israel to a standard different from the expectation of other states. When some Christian groups express a humanitarian concern for Palestinians beyond what they express for any other suffering human beings, it is understandable that Jews may question their motives.

It is certainly troubling that Israel rules over millions of unwilling Muslim and Christian Arabs. Assignment of blame for the situation requires an understanding of the history that has brought us to this point. Assigning blame seldom leads to progress. The search for realistic and humane solutions is a complex challenge that is set back by one-sided charges against Israel. Ultimately, Christian-Jewish reconciliation has to deal with anti-Zionism along with anti-Judaism and anti-Semitism. It seems to me that many supporters of the Palestinians have settled upon a strategy that it is easier to arouse hatred towards the Jewish state than it is to arouse sympathy for the plight of Palestinians. This is unfortunate. Hopefully the strategy of hate-mongering will fail and be succeeded by a strategy of promoting mutual understanding and outcomes that are the best possible for all concerned.

Many Evangelical Christians are strongly supportive of the State of Israel. This support often hinges on beliefs about the coming End of Time. Evangelical support often comes without any recognition of political rights for Palestinians, since God has promised the Land of Israel to the Jewish people alone. It seems that most Christians support or oppose the State of Israel for theological reasons of their own which have very little to do with the Jewish concerns that led to the Zionist movement. Jews and Christians view Israel – "the Holy Land" through different lenses.

Academic scholarship in the study of religion has both reflected and caused huge advances in Christian-Jewish relations. Since the dawn of the Enlightenment, Christian scholars have studied Christian origins while Jewish historians studied the origins of Rabbinic Judaism. The scholars often failed to communicate because one group studied mostly texts in Latin and Greek while the other studied texts written in Hebrew and Aramaic. It eventually dawned on all these historians that Christian origins and Jewish origins are one and the same subject. In our times there is great cooperation between historical scholars which has led to both greater self-understanding and greater mutual understanding between Jews and Christians.

Jewish Studies has become a standard department in secular and Christian universities. Multitudes of non-Jewish students take a college course on Judaism as part of their undergraduate studies. Besides Introduction to Judaism there are courses on the Holocaust, on Kabbalah, on Jewish philosophy, on Jewish literature, and many other topics of general interest. Jewish-Christian Relations has become an academic topic in itself, with many brilliant scholars holding academic chairs in this specific subject area. For decades before the 1960's, Jewish and Hebrew studies were place in a Department of Oriental Studies, which was a sort of academic backwater for the study of peoples and cultures deemed inferior. Jews strove to have Jewish studies placed into the primary curriculum. This effort has succeeded. The availability of college courses on Judaism and on Christian-Jewish relations is a positive development.

With an end to the accusation of deicide, an end to replacement theology amongst most Christians, an end to missionary activities aimed specifically at Jews except among some Fundamentalist denominations, and an increase in mutual study between Jews and Christians, it is clear that the future of Jewish-Christian relations will not resemble the past. A brighter and happier future beckons. There are many challenges to religion in the contemporary world which Jews and Christians will face together.

Jews in America have our own issues with assimilation and low birth rates and the search for meaning within our own religion. A significant Jewish presence in America, this land of freedom, is not assured. It is good to know that we Jews will work out our present issues in an atmosphere of Christian-Jewish relations more positive than the world has ever known.